W9-DDU-964

COLLECTED
POEMS
Volume II

COLLECTED POEMS
Volume II

RALPH GUSTAFSON

1987

Sono Nis Press

VICTORIA, BRITISH COLUMBIA

Canadian Cataloguing in Publication Data

Gustafson, Ralph, 1909-
  Collected poems

  ISBN 0-919203-77-9 (Vol. 1)
  ISBN 0-919203-79-5 (Vol. 2)

  I. Title.
  PS8513.U78A17.1987   C811'.52   C87-091342-5
  PR9199.3.G8A17 1987

Publication financially assisted by the
Canada Council Block Grant Program.

Published by
SONO NIS PRESS
1745 Blanshard Street
Victoria, British Columbia V8W 2J8

Designed and printed in Canada by
MORRISS PRINTING COMPANY LTD.
Victoria, British Columbia

For Betty

Contents

1982 GRADATIONS OF GRANDEUR

1977
CORNERS IN THE GLASS

It was pleasant to be sitting there,
While the sultriest fulgurations, flickering,
Cast corners in the glass.
—WALLACE STEVENS

Wednesday at North Hatley

It snows on this place
And a gentleness obtains.
The garden fills with white,
Last summer's hedgerow
Bears a burden and birds
Are scarce. The grosbeak
Fights for seeds, the squirrel
Walks his slender wire.
There is a victory;
The heart endures, the house
Achieves its warmth and where
He needs to, man in woollen
Mitts, in muffler, without
A deathwish, northern, walks.
Except he stop at drifts
He cannot hear this snow,
The wind has fallen, and where
The lake awaits, the road
Is his. Softly the snow
Falls. Chance is against him.
But softly the snow falls.

Schubert, I Think It Was, I Was Listening To

Night is interlaced in the leaves,
The long path of the sun is ocean-gone.
Quiet is descended on this house,
Europe and its uses have no province
Here, commerce is forgotten.
This music
Holds every nuance of the attentive heart.
I would not have it otherwise,
You alone and this house,
This quiet, history left to its envy,
Life less each hour.
Time, the years,
Are as the emotion of this night—
Apart, alien as stars now
Among the leaves seen from this window,
The world travelled, its streets inconsequent,
Each man his centre of arrogations,
And still this music to be heard;
This quiet here with stars,
A grace acknowledged, this coming night
A short loss
Before tomorrow's rising up of sun.

Morning's Light

Even the suffering's worth it.
When the ground-phlox blooms
What of the pain; there is cessation;
The jonquil is white, the oriole
Sings? No? Then surely there is
Remembrance, that first ecstasy?
Music dwells in the soul.
Perhaps that first hearing of Sibelius'
Tuonela, or even at dawn
Something as simple as that oriole,
Liquid, crazy with love heard
In the far garden, the elm by the lake's
Side, intuitive with lopsided possession
And morning and sun and love.

There is a sobering beyond all
Comprehension. It is this leaving
Of suffering, of birds, oriole and elm
And remembrance and lake's side,
And hearing of music.

Of Green Steps and Laundry

The man will put a large-headed nail,
Shiny as silver, into the green step,
Straightening winter's bias and spring
Thaw and his hammer will knock it crooked,
The bird come obtrusively to the bough above,
And it will have to be done again, and that
Will be important; and she will hang
Blue and white shirts and a patched quilt
On the laundry line that runs from the kitchen
Step to the yard telephone pole and sheets
That smell of winter's cold, and the pulley
Each time the line is launched will squeak,
And that will be important; and neither
She nor the man pounding the clear air
Fixing the green step with another nail,
Will be aware of the importance, twenty
Years later thought of by him
Who drove nails and saw laundry,
Who thought little of cardinals and clothespins
And now loves life, loves life.

In Dispraise of Great Happenings

Birdsong and the midge drinking needfully:
Otherwise happenings of summer afternoons.
Such great fountains tumble water
At d'Este. I at the spring unwanted
At the corner of the patio, my foot in it
Unobserved, pull weeds. The choice
Between weedy violet and potential
Ground-phlox massed in May and red
And white and to be propagated, is Troy
Fallen or not, a thing of moment
And momentous choice whether the midge succeed
In swallowing smaller than itself or,
Should birdsong cease? Let Helen
Waddle down the street and be beautiful.
I shall go to bed far later on
And pull the sheet up over time.
Now I watch the cataclysmic gulp
By midges made and conjugate
What question lies in oriole song
Oblivious of Agamemnon and a thousand ships.

The Overwhelming Green

The green was overwhelming,
Verdant or that trembled
Against the sky, the sky
Light blue, a blue
That deepened as the eye
Held on. It would have been
Deprivation not to have
Taken on death to see this.

    It was Godsmart. That.
But best luck also,
Good weather and summer,
Not a day needing litanies—
The usual not usually
Paid much attention to,
The green preponderant over
Probables, the blue bluest,
The last possible, until head
Went down and eyes sought
Relief in burst of peony,
Ordinary, imbricate, civil,
Without inclusions of God
And Paternity and supernal
Intimations—there
To be looked at, used, itself,
Common, affianced and adjunct
To a meaning or not, just
As you wished, in love or not
Or however you made the peony
Be because you looked at it
In a certain state because
The song sparrow broke
Into song or over your shoulder,
Should you look up,
A hill with trees and a house,
Or that you had to get on
To something else but meanwhile
Looked at the peony that was there.

Of Cabbages and Pianos

Degas wanted Pissarro to draw
A cabbage. Such beauty in the world,
Such enormity, such cancellations!
Common ground by common consent
To be tread on, outlines of colours,
Crystals of snow undergone!
The placing of a bowl bought in Greece
On a coffee-table, she in a blouse
From Edinburgh kneeled down
To do it in the winter sunlight
Through the window. Challenges, senses
To be devoted to, high metaphysics
To accept or deny that God's done for!
      Summation simple enough: to have life,
Domesticities, her centering
A kylix brought from Olympia; with love
Dusting under the lid of a grand
Piano! that winter-sun across her,
Gluck's "Mélodie" from *Orpheus* transcribed
By Sgambati on the music rack
Before her silent.
           We have heard
Cicadas transcribed by moon, and other
Many memoirs, the breath of Athena
Left in her flute found by Marsyas
Flayed and classical commitments to cabbages
Made. All complications of simple
Summation, the worst and best of these:
Death thought of, Degas dead;
And the world to be praised in resultant cabbage.

Sermon for the Day

The cobweb strung between two stones
To catch food. And will you live
Only a season, spider? After
All that bumwork, beauty without
Brain, delicacy designed for stomach,
What of your destiny, slipshod
As your web isn't? I
Could blow it apart. So God loved
The world He gave us brevity in it.
Cynicism isn't up your alley.
But you make me think, this web
Your uttermost so you can last
It out. Let us bring flimsiness
To great conclusion: eating flies,
The spider in his web; solid
Certainties that threads can do it.

The Moment Is Not Only Itself

Raking leaves, putting them in bags,
Stooped over, green gloves on—
The whole of it suddenly Chopin's Prelude
In E♭ major. You know it? *Vivace.*
Legato e sempre leggiero?
Difficult, intricate, melody
As outside the possibility of this world
Of heaviness as want of it. Not
Ache of muscles of the wrists unused to the
Stretches put me in mind of it.
Shoving leaves into tilted bags
Is easy enough, no strain on what
Fingers can do though not brought
To sensitive answer by a lifetime's agony—
That is, joy—the same thing,
The music gained thought worth it; or
Those hands, width, stretch, joint,
Apart from what sheer will can bring them
To, actually physiologically
Born to eighty-eight keys of such
And such a width and space, astoundingly
Matched to the world's manufactury.
Not to be accounted for, miracles. I
Leaned over to get autumn in bags
And suddenly it was April. It
Was October, almost the end of it.
Air was gentle up from the lake,
It smelled of branches, there was a crow's caw,
The sun was hot. It was spring, so.
Perhaps that was the craziness brought Chopin
In my head, that Prelude when
The year was finished. Affiance fools
The brain. As in love often.
What is real is what the heart
Has. Old leaves in green
Bags are beginnings with the wind right,

Chopin in your head. What chose
To have it there is your own doing.
My guess is the way the senses
Are lived. Not to deny autumn
Its own glory, dead leaves
Affirming April are what you've loved
Brought to bear: high mindings,
Signals of thought, code of body
Made exquisite and tall doings,
Structures of devotion that make the end
Of foliage, of summer, descendings—however
You finish it—not matter.

Trio for Harp and Percussion

I *Argument*

If God is the speed of light,
As well crack walnuts set
At table. If so,
Golgotha is an abstract thought
And Light's speed dug in toes
And shoved a plane at Nazareth.

I'll have the concrete.

                    From here
To there, quicker than a wink.
There, where's there?
Infinitum. Einstein,
Asked, fiddled. So
Do I. I'll have a measure of music,
A bolt of good concordance,
Heard notes,
Above ground.
Lay me down in time
I'll think of speed.

Light, Erigina's Light
(Capital L)'s
An abstract absolute.
I'll have sun
On cranky crystal, corners in
The glass, tablecloths and silver,
Oranges with peels on them,
Crack inconsequential nuts
And talk of music,
Haydn; light my own
Apocalyptic candle.

II   *Adagio ma non troppo*

As who shall sit in the sun
Thinking himself immortal,
Rameses in his chair,
His face broken, Tiye
That Nubian queen come
To Egypt done by the sculptor
In jasper hardest after
Diamond, beauty gone,
Only lips left,
The reach of river, dust.
The barge she sat in, like a
Burnish'd throne . . . Starry
Cassiopeia, lady
With her mirror in
The sky where physics sits
Dispensing laws. I'll
Have earthly music, heard,
Unsphered, no choirs squeaked
In eternal passacaglia
As the planets turn
In need of oil but mortal
Tribulations, that *Festspiel*
Seat hard on the bottom
For sweet acoustics' sake,
Wagner delving his gold
E♭, and sweeter, Schubert
Dying of Eros, handing
The theme that summer in Steyr
To amiable Krump, his bull-fiddle
Less than immortal, Kathi,
Large blue eyes, thick
Gold tresses, upright in
Her chair while papa gives
A dubious *A*, the short-lived
Schubert full of smiles.

III   *Diabelli Variations*

Beethoven's *schusterfleck*, a cobbler's
Patch: magnificence! Sole of a shoe,
Hermes' sandal; skullcap, halo;
Digested mushroom, Helen's shoulder;
Earth a heaven! Well, not quite.
But what the world can do in time!
Transmogrification, mud bedaubed,
Bedizened! Botticelli's girl,
Canvas, paint and camel hair;
James' Bible, glue and ink—
Metamorphosis manipulated
By eardrum, pulse and pate! So,
Diabelli asked Beethoven,
"Ein variation on mein liddle
Theme." Thirty-three! Inanity
Brought sublime, empyrean reached,
Become his last sonata, Beethoven
Deaf!
        Instances, exaltations,
Mortalities—apostrophes at
Their ends! Why not? Any son
Of divinity can rub his nose in dust
If so inclined, a beneficial
Exercise—but not the whole of it,
Fix and finish yet, not
By a longshot, mankind notwithstanding:
Jesus and His lousy deal,
Jonah ducked, Pound pitched
In a loony bin and Liszt betrayed—
The Saturday sundry of this world,
Schumann mad, hearing *A*,
Schubert turned to the wall to die.

Husks and blossoming, sun and mud.
No help for it.

        At Bonn, in a case,
Ear-trumpets against the stars.

Partial Argument

Poetry, the only act which separates
Truth from supposition. Atomic
Missive is accurate but supposes. Music
Is pure: F-sharp, F-natural,
Without burdens such as "we
Must love one another or die"
Or thirteen million a year are born
In India. The greater art, but
Itself. Poetry, the truth
Plus trouble. Let us suppose the polished
Lens discovers a black star,
The rocks on the moon are shoved back
A billion years. Does Jack love
Jill?
     No, I tell you, the poet's
Postulate trembles with extents,
The writing's urgence is a doctor's script,
The sculptor's inch, *that* much comparison.
Kitchen statistics mark the loaf and
Knead of bread but I have seen
Coition with belly hunger-bitten
Predicted by a verse, the farthest
Decimal relay supposition
And oil from Persia choke birds.
"Instinctive integrations" lacking,
The day's absurd; clocks are compassion;
The world's measure taken by honest
Men, an iridio-platinum
Metre at 62°.
Words in a poem come together
Implacably as an apple tastes;
A pond, a dog, three boys on skates;
Someone singing or a death.

30

Poetic Poem

The blunder is not to stain
Your hand in actual pollen,
Twirl a beater in egg,
Crush strawberry on your palate fine.

Walk down more streets
Staring in store windows, prose joints,
Emporia of fresh leather shoes
Shineable after slick mud.

This is the world, with red sunsets,
A star in them, green mown grass,
A hankering after the feel of peeled hickory
Or the feel of a sudden axiomatic thought.

That man puts his hat back on sorrowfully
Staring after someone he thought he knew.
Coming across real poetry, owls hoot,
Potatoes break ground, and coffee smells.

Phases of the Present

I Prelude

A minor planet on the edge of an
Insignificant system in a
Galaxy accountless in an
Immoderacy of stars—of course
It's important. I look up, a bit
Out of focus, my spectacles off,
The whole world is green
And blue, sun blazes
And a yellow ash leaf
Falls in my lap. I am
In a garden on the edge
Of nowhere, life and death
In my lap. Of course it's important.

II The Newspaper

That photo of the little Jew in the cap,
Back to the gun held by the Nazi
With splay feet aware of the camera,
The little boy his hands in the air,
I turn over. I don't want to see it.
As a member of the human race. I am
Civilized. I am happy. I flap the
Newspaper with the picture over
So that when it is picked up to be taken
Down cellar to be put with the trash
I won't see it. I am sensitive.
The little boy is dead. He went
Through death. The cap is his best one.
He has brown eyes. He does not
Understand. Putting your hands
Up in front of a carbine prevents
The bullet. He is with the others.
Some of them he knows, so
It is all right. I turn
The paper over, the picture face
Down.

Mothy Monologue   —*Matthew* VI, 19

The moth flew a bee-line,
The flame beckoned but there was
A globe around it. The moth acted
Drunk after. My heart went
Out.

    That Phnom-Penh child
Bombed in the stairway looks like a roast of
Meat—except for the arms and legs.

Moths don't fly bee-lines.

This one did. All the way back
To Moscow.

      The cellar stairs all
Are lined with human meat.

            This,
In times of truce...

        My heart goes out.

At least all the little children
Are dead reasonably.

      Insurgent
Howitzers are within killing
Distance of the kindergarten...

So what's new?

      Well, let's see,
The Khmer-Rouge should exempt those
Not near burial details.
The smell crosses the Pacific.

Of course,
Hanoi is absolutely right.
So is Saigon.

My heart goes out.

Then again, the world's population
Is explosive. A village a day
Is born in India.

For infant mortality,
Thank God.

The globe is where I study.
Guerillas prevent my seeing
Angkor Wat. I have been down
The Chao Phya River, though,
Where the poor are happy—or seem happy—
Pounding laundry on the bank stones,
And jumping in the river, the kids.
Maybe we better leave Thailand
Alone. The hut coming next
Sports a TV aerial... I'm drifting
Down the river on a sugar boat.
I travel this way, my own
Sweet way. I don't like
Guided tours...

To return to my study:

Eastward, the world is rich with oil.
They are jacking Israel from the sands of time.

I better sign off.

I smell
Something burning.

IV *Bestiary*

At the trough and then the urinal,
A mighty magnificence is mankind.
Nature has us stumped. Spirit's soiled.
Listen to him rant then consider
These two colts in fettle, they push
Not, neither do they pretend.
Or ponder this baboon, it does not
Laugh too loudly at its own jokes
Nor go to Helsinki to give away
Patrimony, it is tolerant of whether God
Is coconut or banana,
It is a very Christian soul,
Not feeling virtuous through hate.
The cat, sleek, washes itself.
It is a dignified domain. Ducks
Stand naturally on their heads, swans
Are silent and dying, the elephant
Seeks privacy, does not trumpet
Imperfection and go to the moon.
Pre-eminently the spider is openly subtle.
Even Death
Seeks various considerate ways to make
His ever appealing presence known.

V   *Rondo*

Yah! Yah! caterwauling
Hales the world,
Mush of language,
Third to tonic third to
Tonic third to tonic
Sends the host,
Hair hides the undistinguished.
Adolescence screams.
Balance of payments swells.
Democracy levels. Detergents
Propagate.
At 8 o'clock Niagara Falls
Breaks out in colours.

Meanwhile

Syllabic Jocko
Hiccoughs on his wire,
By his dentures slides to earth.

Blue City

The air is quiet
and the window
holds a truce
with the sun
red
where it went down.
The sill is dust.
This is
a dirty city.
Blacks sing in the dusk
slowtime.
They have invaded
the neighbourhood
with harmony,
greatchords
like sorrow,
a broken armchair,
TV, bedsprings,
junk
on the street,
and the universe
constructed of stars.

*The Lord God was hung
on the lonesome tree*

they sing in the dusk.

In Sight of Etna

Etna, cone of snow. And oleander,
Paths of oleander, pink and sweet-smelling,
Fields of wheat, copper-gold and windblown
Bronze, bronze against green, the green of olive,
Silver-green the Mediterranean; over the island,
Cone of snow. We stand on ashy
Desolation, crust beneath our feet.
Harsh contrast! gods demolished, great Zeus
His temple down that Agrigento had,
The green valley shaken. Empedocles
Leaps in, incinerates himself to show
Himself a god—the earth unfinished where Etna shrugs.

Stucco and Salamanders

Poseidon's pillars transported, stuck
In a Christian nave, the crimson dot
(The right-hand monstrance at the end of the plaster
Aisle next to the porcelain Mary)
Burning transubstantiation.
Pagan beauty appropriated,
The altar-linen scrubbed in the galvanized
Tubs of Paestum.

                    Across the fields,
Poseidon's realm, ocean's salty
Smell, sun and stones given
Over to the slick salamander.

Paestum, That Place of Lovely Temples

The green-eyed goddess nimble and passionate
Invests this place, Athena in Compania;
Vines and olives her sister Ceres
Looks after. Far cry,
Rome and Saint Peter's worn-down toe!
Here thirty columns drenched two thousand
Years in setting suns support
Nothing. On the *Via de' Fiori* the cripple
Syncopates a cockcrow church;
Down the aisle before a bleeding
Christ mixed up with tourists, suppliance
Raises prayers.

          Contrasts! This
With that. The drilled heart so
Accepts didactics, sun on marble
Is detraction, loveliness
A penance, the nimble goddess
Sorrow in a gilded field.

The Sun on the Temple Was Gold

Nine years, nine, since we
rode donkeys up to Lindos first.
Light bathes the broken columns,
blue the Aegean, a mile down,
the Acropolis bathed in sun where
they came with flute and sheaves. Nine
years, the temple-stairs to the sun,
the sea windswept, the same.

I think of the ninth hour, time
not to be redeemed, that lost
hour His last... Saint Paul's cove
down there puts the remembrance
in mind. Where the curve is green,
the sheltering rock below the shallower
water, green, that hard man stepped...
But blue, blue the Aegean...

                      I turn to
Helios and thoughts of her, patient
in her ribboned hat against
the shadowed sandstone pillar
elsewhere golden there, Helios
his descendent light, mine, and love.

Words for a Resurrection

And unicorns broke cover
and all the copse was covered with crocus.
This was in autumn when finches munch gravel
and satyrs acorns
which make them mad.

A queer time, an odd *pendule*
and waggle of pendulum.

But I thought of the crisis of Pan
and the tone of *F* minor when
someone yelled: *Great Pan is dead!*

... moss stuffed his ears as he rolled
as he came and he didn't hear.
Sex was more.

Unicorns grazed unafraid of the coming

and all the sunsets blazed in an uprising.

Canto for Pan

Out of his coming paeans ring.
In a circle the snowdrops, already
Under the snow a wheeling of witness
Working for sun. Sun! Buds stiffen
And branches are sticky with sheathing
On petals that thrust and will colour spring!
Still muddy the soil, but crimson
Tipping the shove of peony at top of
The garden steps. Bells hang round
And pendulums wring down scales off the
Male-hung fir. Wind senses
Lapsing of snow-smell now unravelled
As time unravels all things borne.

Ladies Lovely

All of history plunged through.
And is she dead and how
Through that portal? with cries
And terror, that beautiful lady, Aquitaine,
Or was she shrewish then, the court
Glad to get rid of her? And Gloriana dying.
Standing up for fifteen hours, her breath
Intolerable to be near and the
Spanish ambassador quashed.
And Egypt that lovely who brought off
Fifty at dinner, and died
Black in the face from the snake,
        O what of them,
How did they sustain that going,
The golden-braided girl of Sandro,
Sweetness passionate? And Lola with a pistol,
Liszt worn out.
Hard to think of Jenny now a skull,
Boadicea dust—
But she wasn't pretty,
Beefsteak yelling in a bladed car—
And yet a lady to some great slobbering oaf.
Oh well. Boucher's darling,
Miss O'Murphy on her tummy,
Modest inner thigh apart for Louis.
All love and dust!
Got-through humiliation.
London bridge as well as ladies.
Gone. All of them. A poem left.
Indignity gone through,
Lovely ladies, lovely ladies.

Nefertiti

Nothing compares. Nefertiti
Breathing. I saw her swallow—
That daring neck, poise
For the heavy crown
Of blue, above the forehead
Uraeus coiled; royal,
Unknown except through love.
Hands of the sun have given
The breath of life. Achet-Aten,
How beautiful the city that could hold
Such beauty, a detail in
The cluttered shop of Tuthmose, unfinished
In a corner of the room.
Two-timing time ready
With Egypt's sand.

        In love
With plaster on a core of stone!
Segesta, Parthenon, hunky
Moore, our welded scrap,
What, to her chin and lips?
I watch elegance, all else,
Vulgar time.
She smiles or seems to smile.
Inscrutable as grace.

Of Cordwood and Carmen

Stacking wood to broadcast "Carmen."
Dumped in the driveway four runs
Of birch to keep in front of the fireplace
Warmth, and her in the basement
Piling the future, gloves and purple tuque
And topboots on, disposition as ever
Not a hurt
Towards anyone's life. Arranging wood,
She hums offkey with Bizet,
Love and that spade, the ace of Death.
Death, what hope for you!
Up through the floor I listen
To clunking cutwood birch stained with snow.
Outside, a copper sun; branches black
Against the coming snow. Day
Sets and not many to count.
She hums.

Song for Next Lent

If life weren't grim with suffering
It would be hilarious—look at
That footprint left on the moon
That won't grow a radish, and
Those fields of corn the man with the pot-belly
Walks over; the golden horn
The hunt blows, roast fox
For supper while redneck has his dinner
Midday from his pail. I
Have seen yesterday's newspaper on
The floor of subways caught in time.
Once a year ago, my wife and I
Travelled nine days up the Nile
To see a painted tomb. Christ hung
Nine hours, so we are told. Hilarious
How the centuries go. Only Good Friday
Past, the sirens sang across Green Park
And Schicklgruber had his day. Ticklish
Sobriety, though, the cloth and grind it took
To polish Palomar's lens so we could site
A vacuum. Children starve,
Tin plates in their hands in Sunday
Supplements. A thousand humorous
Presentiments begin to rise...
      Oh well. Laugh. Silently. I hear
The larkspur in the bush and sap
Begins in maple trees to rise.
My la-ady sweet arise, arise,
Arise. My la-ady swee-eet
Arise. *Tum ta.*

The Exact Worth of Trusting Sunlight

The sun is hot, the sofa
By the window the place to be,
One lid closed against it while
You read so razzle-dazzle
Is it. But don't depend on it.
One moment now I shut
My eyes, blind gold and promising
Patches gilt-edged crawling
Genetics on the sobersides
Like Darwin on the *Beagle*
Finding apes. The next
(Moment) dark fell down,
The page of poems of dazzle-razzle
Done in, the sun gone in.
If seeking injunction, turned-over
Stone and old tin cans filled
With coins, washed-up gems and offhand
Goldbricks, move across the room
There in umbrageous alcove safe
From revocable sun and shades snapped up
On April mornings, pails of worms
For pastel fish and other
Horrendous fizzle.

Equivalence

An overplus of stars!
More than I need.

1978
SOVIET POEMS

Red Square

A half moon with a star above it,
Silver, just upward of the moon
When it should be below, the star as usual;
Both above the citadel, the kremlin
Wall silent where the heroes
Are, ashes who made the great square
Red, *krasnaya*, where Lenin lies.
Moonlight floods the Square. We
Before Saint Basil's, God gone,
Between the grounded mind and what it
Wills, intercession not needed.
Faithful, Basil's clustered churches,
The nine, nestled in their past,
Domes and towers, twisted blue
And gold, knotted crimson washed
By the servile moon; intuitive cleave
And clearance, one articulation
Only, as they who built it blinded
So there could not be another.
Beauty not to be commanded,
Or tomb or hero not to be,
Briefness fulfilled as we stand here.

The Old Moscow Woman

The woman this morning sweeps the pavement
Of Kuibysheva Street,
Branches of spring tied to an old stick,
Brushing along last night's bits
Of paper, cigarette ends, dirt,
Keeping the city clean for this morning's
Traffic. By night it will have to be done
All over again. She looks happy.
What is this happiness? Grandchildren,
Soup on the stove, an hour's relief
From pain, Lenin sleeping nearby?
The street will always be dirty.
Mankind is imperfect.
Politics and bad manners
Leave his detritus
On the perfect peace. We
Do not understand one another.
The street will have to be swept again.
New York, Moscow, Montreal,
It is the same. Man is careless,
He drops the wrappings from his hands,
The torn paper, even the newspaper
With the news of the world
He leaves behind him to be picked up
By someone else. The wind is cold.
This is September. Soon the snow
Will cover the shivering gutter
And the plough will supersede the broom.
We all feel it. No matter the labour.
Snow and death come.
Do they not?
And yet this woman sweeps,
For a few kopeks,
Lentils for her soup,
And is happy.
What is this Moscow?
This humanity?

Memorial Gun on Gorky Street

—on a line in Blok's poem, "The Twelve"

Like the old crone and the political banner
From house to house across the street
Whose cloth otherwise
Could keep children warm,
I look at the military hardware
Monumental in the plaza.
I am reminded of other hardware
In the arms of girls,
Rusted irony.
The detonator won't pull,
The screw accommodation is
Too worn for firing.
The old crone is right.
A pair of scissors,
Expenditure cut down
Might scare up some money for
A few orange lollipops for the children.
Happiness is not hard to come by,
It is not expensive.
What of the filing-cabinets, you say?
The erasers and
Duplicate copies?
Where would the papers be
Not in alphabetical order?
Responses would falter,
Accords would fail.
Turn banners into baby-linen,
Balances of advantage,
Peace, would disappear.
What of the chocolates for the children?

Moscow Circus

Midair, four and four
(The figure Jung said expressed
The ultimate divine reality within us)
The figures of the four girls,
The four guys, spangled,
Walking the tightrope,
Flaw each side of them across
The tent top, birth to death,
Equilibrist, each toe delicate
Set in front, Natasha upside down
On Vasily's head. Strobe
Lights play, drum
Points, the whole Copernicus put
On a step... She's pretty. He,
Axiom. They reach the platform,
Whirl, salute the world.
Next time, next time:
Misunderstanding,
Slackened love...

Night, Samarkand

We flew with the sun into the sun
Lying low on the wide horizon
Like a disc of copper metal
Thrown by luck. Later, the moon,
Half itself, washed silver the walls
Of the sapphire Schools where silence
Is, blue, glazed, across
The court, the leaning minaret;
Each side, archways, glossed,
Paved with scripted gold
The inner traves, portals starry
As the milky way—that stare on
Present brick. We stood in the shadow.
The dog beside the broken pavement
Scratched fleas, slant posts
Lugged wire to the flooding lights.
                    In moonlight,
Touching their foreheads with their palms,
In prayer the two old men mourn
The future of the hopeful past.

Tolstoy's Estate

Of accommodations there is no end:
Tolstoy who laboured in the field with the peasants,
The footman at his door;
"Master, the plough is ready."

St. Cyril's, 12th Century

What wonders cease when we are
Casual and indifferent
To simple faith.

I climb the church stairs
Within the crude wall
And come on God

In the likeness of others' love,
Arches bend roughly coloured
With ancient saints.

Nonsense, I say, a waste
Of emotion; hurt and
Grief unanswered.

I am rebuked. What comfort
Of theirs do I know of?
What crying ceased?

I wander the balcony of
The church with my faith
In nothing and poems.

I see the end of arrogance,
On the walls, trumpets sound,
The angel rolls up the sky.

The Skull Beneath the Skin

I saw one thousand nine hundred and seventy-six
People waiting to get into Lenin's tomb,
Tartar, Russian, Uzbek, Kasakh and
Canadian, some carrying purses,
Some, cameras, some wore kerchiefs,
Some inhabited uniforms, I saw children,
The wise, those once-suffered, the old, each
In line, moved slowly, moving between
White lines drawn on the pavement
To get into the tomb, one thousand
Nine hundred and seventy-six, one thousand
Nine hundred and seventy-six skulls,

In the Cathedral

On the pulpit, mounting its stairs,
The martyrs carved in gilt
Wood, rococo each with his
Axe, his saw, all
Subservient to God,
God everywhere
In the Dom, arch and aisle,
In the instructed heart, the listeners
Still, below; organ
Vast with sound, pipes
Vertical to heaven.
O concert in the Dom!
Sweetly Schubert sounds.
Gracious, Handel's pace.
At Jurmala the tide come in.
For a moment, here,
The purpose of martyrdom.

On the Road to Novgorod

Grass white where the shadows are,
On brake and hummock, the forest-road.
The highway to Novgorod. The log
Houses warm. The sun cold.
The birch frosted. At the coppice edge,
Potatoes harvested, bent red
The women's kerchiefs, a hundred along
The field-rows; in the pickup, melons
From Tashkent, on the road-warning,
Running children from anywhere.
While we pass, the old woman
Interrupts her cow, the hunch
Of ground starlings takes off.

And coming home, crimson dusk,
At the edge of the distant woods a house,
Smoke from the chimney, a lighted room.

By Way of Postlude

Prescriptive optimism in all things,
One gets weary of official virtue,
Pictures of good workers on the wall,
Red Star over the avenues,
Church, billboards, exile, toothpaste—
Sick of piety always
There first. Where the ease
From branded presumptions of the future, laughter,
The natural factory, the unstatistical labour?
O the heroic statue, the striding
Into the dawn, the sword raised victorious!
O modesty, not higher, not bigger.
Nothing is wrong here liberty
Won't cure.

      And yet,

O Russia, O Uzbekistan and Ukraine,
Latvia. Where more generosity,
Where more honourably glorious dead,
More friendship and giving? The strictures,
They would not come at all if not
From love, I would not write this down
Not aware of freedom's own failures,
The poet not his own revolution.

I stand again in Red Square,
The goose-stepping exact guard gone,
Lenin left alone, the half moon
At eleven, over St. Basil's,
The Place of the Forehead, the round ukase
Empty, the stones of the Square immaculate
With night. My mind fills,
Those three weeks, poems the successors...

Quiet with admonitions the time-zones,
The Rockies white with glaciers under
The Moscow moon, these silent bells
Heavy with burdens of Canadian snows.

1979
SEQUENCES

Winter Sequence

I   *Without Renunciation of South*

Of the passions, of the amassing harmonies
Let the absolute South be symbol as it may.
Here is winter, the crystal snow
Is a silence, from the shaken bough
Cascades of heaven's anonymity
And rushing white
Pummel sensations. The soft South
Is attended to, sands pile at Pyla,
Persia has her pomegranate,
Carib waters break on permanent
Hot beaches, that pulsing pleasure "schifanoia"
Has been pursued
And the heart comes home to the North;
The thought passionate, the chancery of winter,
As much a harbinger.
Reverse the myth, than winter
No truer paraclete warbles in his jungle,
Yukon is a magnificence,
Harmonies of autumn proclaim
Enduring love.

II

The snow drives all one way,
The wind is from the west.
Seasons become one
Awareness; bud is apple
And all things grow round
With attainment—given fair
Luck; fire burns
Birch in the midst of winter
And that same ripeness which is locked
In round apples is
Locked crisp white
In thickening seven-feet
Snow. O as beasts
Tense, thrust, sleep,
We last the seasons—if chance
Is fair, not knocking hurt
Into appletime nor dipper
Of clear water down
Fronts. We could do
Without change, winter
Finding us out. But now
The snow drives one way,
The chill wind eastward,
The heart contends with irony
So many seasons accurate
To themselves have come
And gone. Fulfilment brings
Love boundary. There comes
A time (earth tilted
As fairly) when opposites oppose,
Hazards so rounded,
Death does not fail
Nor empires of green and tumbled
Continents redeem
The eastward driving snow.

III

Snow lay along the long bough
As if that could scare birds,
As if constancy were done for. But I doubted
That could scare denizens: I have seen
Sparrows scrabbling, a squirrel indifferent,
In the arms of drifts; conversely,
Day brought up short in summer's
Term and an hour later, sky
That was rubbed silver dazzling
The eye, struck across dark
Winter. The mind knows that music
Will never stop. The constancy is,
Who will hear it? Sadness lies
Beneath all music. Four seasons
Are not enough. The heart, paced,
Halts, birds sing and die in time
Not knowing it. But there's the dignity!
The mind's apart. Seeing creation
Cease, we stand on eminences knowing it,
Look back on brevities, ahead to lost
Fortunes, so that we know renewals. A crux
Not got out of. Except these lungs stop.
(Yes, I have seen men eased out indifferently,
Birds stupid on winter boughs.)

IV

It was a full moon, a circle,
Not a spheroid, a perfect circle,
A complex of bare branches
Up across it where the slant
Of the hill is; so clear,
So sharp the moon, the ice golden
On the lake was a summer exactness
Though the bare branches were winter.
She drew my attention to it,
Calling that I must see, on the verandah.
Love is attentive: to every burn
Of a red glass sun through it;
Every thrust of wet green,
The garden usual with the look
Of March familiar with leaves fallen;
Each moon a rising gold
To look at. Love is aware,
Knowing, even the night sharp,
Cold on the winter air, that ice and
Moon looked-at are certain,
Still and happening and not again.

V

The river ice is thin, the wedge
Where the current is is sharp,
A silver knife against the sun.
Trees wait. The pond gathers—
Up beyond the cold-loving
North bank, colour of smoke
Now, having had all the months
Of winter. Thawings are everywhere.
Design stirs.

        Perversely,
He would cancel promises, have winter
In love with nothing, long stars
Of April all very well,
But river ice, closings-over
Where roots are, are rid of announcements,
Implications, betrayals. Honesties,
He would be in love with those.

VI

Final snow falls and branches
Wait. The mantel above the hearth
Where blossoms of forsythia are placed is bare.
I listen to Liszt's "Funérailles",
The world white and that swift passage
Not only to spring, learned.
My heart turns to her, turns
From elegy. Beautiful the music, the snow
Falling, the inescapable hour.

Country Walking

I

Two humps of snow stood on two fir trees,
The place looked like an entrance to importance,
To a field of white snow, field
As in heraldry, leading nowhere of much
Consequence, a slope with a cottage on it
Shut up for the winter, the roof without icicles,
No one there for a fire. I went between the gates
Of the trees to anywhere. Shadows on the slant
Were purple, prints were in the snow
For no purpose, the denizen apparently
Not caring, going on instinct.
I thought of sophistications, music and poems:
How Liszt solved his fugue
Back into romantic grandeur,
How Yeats shook the desert birds
With emerging beasts of Bethlehem.
The snow was darkening white,
Runnels of shadow unravelling.
It seemed consequence was forgotten.
I looked back then upward, to scuffing clouds.
I went on across the hastening light,
My weight pressing in, leaving
Footprints, a complication into.
Suddenly
Sun slammed through going.

II

As you go up the road you will notice
That not all the trees are slapped
With snow on the north bark-side,
The south wind up the lake
Is also bitter on days that are not
Still, redpolls feed on the road
Only with ruffled comfort. Farther
Up the hill you will look at
Caps of snow undisturbed
On the upright posts of the snakefence
Slants. The hill here is protected
By a higher rise of fir and bare
Aspen. As you go down, slowly
Black Point swings by and the lake
Appears. The spread snow on the ice
Is formally patterned by the wind in strokes
Of parallel shade as if some purpose
Was meant. Farther on, just
To the side of you on the white snow open
To sudden sun, green and crimson
Crystals flash, too trivial
To matter, blue also and where red
Impinges, a purple not having
Any regal purpose evident
But the whole refraction so dazzling,
The white and jewelled field,
You raise your eyes. You can always look
Away. The wind here slaps
The cheek and forehead with cold again.
Farther on there is a red barn.
An outdoor double wooden swing
Belongs to the landscape, the apple-barrel
Is tipped over beside the tree,
An abandonment of no use. Beyond,
The place you had headed for proves
Upland too exposed to go to.

You will turn home but notice how
The shadows now hard on the crust
Are broken crossing the ploughed road.
The wind at your back seems to have dropped.
The way home, familiar, always
Seems shorter. The snow creaks.

III

The moon is up there with a cart on it
White-golden. Down here,
Calmly ice on the lake freezes;
The movement of air brushes the cheek
With cold; old Mr. Hall is dying.
There is no concern. Christmastree lights
In places blink green and red
For whatever purposes Eaton's makes of it.
My nose wants to run. Gloves on,
I wait to get home. I want to get home
To my own true love. It is glorious.

Proposition for Gold Trumpets

I

Chekhov's coffined corpse was delivered
To Petersburg in a railway wagon labelled
"Fresh oysters"; Nelson to London
Pickled in a keg of brandy.
Proprieties collapse amid fried
Onions, saucepans, used
Laundry. We walk among indignities,
Imperative excrement along the waters,
Rock and punk blast over
Cathedral entrances, effluents
Inform the air. Yet some households
Put geraniums on window-sills.
I have heard students sing
In Sainte-Chapelle, in narrow alleys
Linen freshly washed announce
The wind. Sad gardens give
Grounds for hope. Not entirely
Flowers held on high by Brezhnev
Despatching tanks behind his smile
At Bratislava, sadden the wind.

71

II

Who reads those doors of Novgorod,
Of Zeno at Verona, who is
Not moved with grace and kingdoms: Noah's
Dove back to the salty window;
Mary brought to bed; Salome
Upside down in dance
For very love? Beaten bronze.
Devotions solve the brassy
World, exactings out of vulgus:
The temple Doric; Suger's nave,
Guildsmen trim with craft;
Backs of the gods, not seen,
The marble carved; honourable pace
Among the hanging stone—the oaten
Stops become Arezzo's scale.

Dignity shapes the vulgar suns
To candle's wick, gloss
Of final vespers.
We beat out going-prayers.
The leaf is gold, Buddha on his elbow;
Zoser in Egypt beneath his stones.

III

Glittering with sun as the wind moved
Were all the leaves of the tree.
It was a concordance between heaven
And the earth. Below, evening fell,
No shadow, but a deepening green.
Birds came and went. The time
Seemed holy though there was no proof,
The leaves trembled in the sun and the tall
Green was standing from some force,
The birds sang for some reason.
It was clear something was at work,
Not only sensation. The man built
The new lattice-work under
His verandah and the sound of nails hammered
Was on the air. Five strokes
And the nail was in. Something was built.
You could hear that. An improvement.
On the upper leaves sun still trembled
Like gold, like beaten gold, and the air
Overhead was darkening blue and the birds sang.

1980

LANDSCAPE WITH RAIN

God does not play dice.
—EINSTEIN

Heaven Is Difficult

        Unsponsored solitude indeed.
Space for a firmament interrupted
By a stubtoe agglomeration.
Stars! Under whose aegis? Not
A whisper from anything but singing angels
Whipped up and stuffed in wishes
By fear of vacuums.

        Unfurnished tenancy,
That or stained-glass trumpets blowing
A brassy fanfare from pointed windows?
Churches, I love 'em too, vasty
Cathedrals and braided Shebas daintily
Footing resting pedestals.

        But edifices
And preparatory coughs from eloquent Mobile
About to speak and solve conundrums?
There's a difference.

        I struggle angels,
Jacob sweating his surplice. What
Shall I plump for? Abstract premises
Or interruptive stardom, buttresses
Butting roofs whose inside glooms
Hold fragilities of colour?

The Absurdity of Not Knowing

Colossal perpetration! Out of this,
Dead, not knowing the reason why
Of black holes stuck in heaven.
There they are, swallowing space
Beyond ingestion while we walk streets,
The universe up to something and Sophie
Buying shoes for sore feet.
Poor Sophie. Poor universe
Not having Sophie know why.
The colossal swirl and mammoth pinpoint,
Children spinning tops, mankind
Screwing openings, birth to incontinency,
Dark about the eyes. Meanwhile
The true and starry heavens going
Somewhere with the reasons.
Redundancy! Infinity turning inside
Out while we eat prunes at breakfast.

A Doubt That Heaven's Sensuous

Doughnuts and cathedrals: parameters
Of beauty. Beauty's hitched to earth;
Wisdom heaven's. I'd be wise
In beauty—though dunking doughnuts every
Breakfast's something too much.
Cavernous forms, spume of shadows!
Better a contemplation of yews,
Cossa's frescoes *schifanoia*,
Carefree April in Ferrara.

Hagia Sophia, Holy Wisdom
Is a tessellated wall.
Buddha can have his bo tree.
I'll have—'I'll have'! Who'll have?
Deathward's in possession. None
The less, hot is hot and ginger,
Though gingerly I miss heaven.

The Things of This World are OK

The interior of the grape is OK,
So is the pleasure from the backend
Of a train, the tracks whizzing back
To *punkt* between soft banks,
Meadow-fence and telephone poles
Clicking past like castanets;
Both are compensation for time
Whizzing even quicker. What
Matters everything, the spiral galaxy
In Andromeda thought of, whirling
Like Saint Katherine on her wheel?
All is martyrology
Except that this tang on the tonsil
Meanwhile is Hamlet and cows
Munching meadows are contentment.

Ramble on What in the World Why

Making a meaning out of everything that has happened,
The there-it-is, plainsong, pitch and pinnacle:
All is blanket-plucking otherwise. My father
Lighted a pipe out in a rowboat on the lake
When he fished and brought up Leviathan on a wormy
Hook, Ahab's pegleg in the belly,
So the watching boy said. Brahms
Percolated coffee, something to fiddle with,
The cup, the pot, the burner, to duck having
To write down music. Meaning is wearying; hammers,
Level, hacking out hunks of marble to raise
Cathedrals. I travel to get out of it to walk in them—
And run slambang into gospels of course,
Pegasus loose and the barndoor slammed.
Berryman took poems and jumped off a bridge.
It all comes down to making oneself one
With sea-slime. Knowing *what* is OK,
It's the why we've got to, the prehensile toes
And all the rest of it, slops, jade and Jesus,
Venice, murder, virgins and music, that counts.

Mid-Atlantic, He Clings to Kindling

This urge upon his mounting soul, height
Magisterial and managed by a wind,
Transcendent take-off fiddling Venus, circling
Samson at his mealy winch—looked into,
Is drunken Noah on his windward raft
Launched by Pilate. Atlantis dived for
At Santorin, Cousteau finds liquid.

Spilled milk, hero for a hairpin, lo!
He writes inverted fugues with either hand
In contradiction; nothing stops him, mortuary
Tables, grub, or green-faced God.
Upright genetive and creaky pump, seeks
Himself between his huff and misty glass.

At Least He Perceives Himself

There's no hope for it. We are done for,
The least jag of a bitten hangnail,
The slow-curving rise of a parabola
Of thought. He's Adam having had Eve,
All desire knocked from him,
Looking around, the round apples
Hanging on the branch like globes of happy
Permanence, the leopard, chin on paws,
Asleep. And he's no more.

                              Happy
Birds, without a prick of perception.

He shifts sitting bare-assed on the sod
Adjusting his balls to comfort. Alas.

But the bee sucks. He watches the tendril.
Above him falls syrupy melody.
He thinks a thought. Perception is perceived.
He sees himself sitting there, hearing birds.

Cathedral Window

Sun shines on glazed glass
Translucent with fire, crimsons
Lash the stone paving,

Light which was before the perception of it
Who built the cathedral, the stained window
Needing suffering,

Noah hammering a plank and Jesse
With a tree in him, windy Christ
Handsome walking water.

Out of Chaos, His Starry Structures

And as Gaudier saw a cat in uncut
Marble, read a Chinese
Glyph at sight, "It's a horse,"
So that-one and the other-one drew a line
Out of the fine clear air and wrote it down,
The silk and britches of Arden Woods,
The halls of Luxor, in it.

Where did Daphnis cut his tune?
Fuller rest his dome?
And as that firebrand touched the lips of Logos,
Eliot took the word, Yeats his phrase,
Out of all tradition Pound his book.

A star-shell over the Western Front, Gaudier.
Break no ointments,
Out of stone
An "arrangement of surfaces" comes.

All the Night on Love Depended

The moon was up, half of it, vague,
White, it could pull no tide,
The last six birds flew south. A red
Boat rocked, the lake never
Still. Lights were come on,
Evening darkening the road, the cars
Driving home, the age without
Grace, itself its own criterion.
O all the night on love depended.
The lights came on, the valley darkening,
In the half light the high birds seeking
The south, cars passing along
The road by the lake never still.

Good Friday

With pierced hands he hung at this very
Noontime hour. They put him up,
Heft on his hands,
The jerk back as the stub went
To the hole. Then the suffering for three
Hours, the words and the drink
Of vinegar in between, the rag
Around his sex. It would be
A wonder if he were the god.
He thought so. He was human.

Enough that there he hung. A sufficient
Phalanx of facts attests, turns history
Back to that. The rest, the god
Business, is human need. To defeat
Death. That got, we can get on
With cruelty, hanging stripped humans
Up, his sacrifice sufficient.

O I am up there loving
Him until he die.

                    Symbol
Of light, questionable god,

                              sufficient
Goodness though we truly die.

Landscape With Rain

I looked at the landscape quickly as though
I had not deserved it. Too much time
Had passed and I had not observed
The flash of colour that the leaves show
As rain falls turning the under
Sides to silver with the weight.
The hills move with translucence.
I was careless how the heart revives,
The sight of a horse standing and how
As the moon goes through the night the resonance
Of silence is without birds or any
Hindrance to completion. Light astonishes
The mind with new wonder at dawn.
     These things are felt with guilt
As the days pass and nothing of them
Has been seen except the concern
Of their going.
          I now walk with suspense,
The going not less real but stopping
An uneven of times with astonishment, getting
Where I have to with adequate concern,
Time shortens very quickly,
But seeing at least how the moss
Is green in patches under the rain
Where the boulder stands exposed and the lake
Is come on grandly swept.

Ramble, On Intimacy

Intimacy is the explanation why
We need God: straw in the crib
And cows chawing cud, the spider
Spinning intricacies on the corner beam;
Sesame sprouting, Mazda's burnishing
Growth; Dionysus' moist   .
Warmth groped—nearness, palpable
To fingers, herehold. Speculate:
Who can engulf, sit upstairs
And think into control zipping suns
And lightyear quasars? He'd need a seat
Nowhere to get a perspective or else
He is it. How then create it if
He is it? And physics won't do,
Astral, electro or dish-antennae
Listening until they're blue in the rims,
We won't accept it. Who got there first,
Who was is what we want who set
The blaze, lit the fuse and blew
The equation, jounced the primordial hot
Potato thirty times the sun
And tossed the thing, the purlieus of heaven
Singed silly, mind-boggling
Light from the Big Bang, sparkling
Stars all over creation. Intimacy.
Distance is for the birds. What
We want's someone close to nail
To a cross, Orpheus out of Hell
No looking back, or Moses soaking
His feet following a hard pull
Up and down Sinai, not pulsars
Pulsing in space. Ghost and substance
Both, of course, is the answer—with stars
Out first, at least they are,

Look in your lens and photograph
The stuff, celestial but real as marbles.
God is intimate doings, jackpots
Of bells, tadpoles into frogs—
Part of the same dumbshow process,
But certainly nothing's as good as Jesus
Come down from His fish-fry to take
A breather with Martha, smelling of must
After a hot day on the Mount.

Centennial for Einstein

Uncertainty took over. The quantum theory
Takes possession, only statistical means
Determines where the iridescent atom
Sets momentum down, exactly lands,
Everything's at tangents. "Now I will
A little tink," says Einstein. Einstein thought.
Probability implies its own consent.
The crystal's coruscations clock the stars;
The mountain streams have amity; Beethoven writes.
"God does not play dice," Einstein said.
God nods His beard, mumbles, "The orderly
Harmony of all that exists," and goes to bed.

Praise of Margins

And of the white moon (be praised, O Lord)
—SAINT FRANCIS OF ASSISI

The egret debugs the cows in Grenada,
The white egret perambulating
His dinner as *naucrates ductor* does
His shark. Ocean teems; on land
The tanager wings a million lice.
All is one to Brother Francis.
Love's the pivot; otherwise
Is scales and hair. By that, least
Is most, this worn and dusty challenge
Thereby mock of sequestration
Nor the forfeit for redemption.
Praise to the weevil who lives on seeds,
Whose nosy head's prolonged to snout;
To the sidling crab compliment.
All is news of God; sequestered
Moon, exaltation. Laud
To the burdened yak who has no need
To shorten breath on mountains, the padded
Cat. Daystream magnify.
God's His least thing, not
To be given up to be got to. Dusky
Day awakes with praise, threadbare
Worms rejoice at starry night.

Variation on a Poem of Montale

*happiness ... It's not for us
and he who has it doesn't know
what to do with it.*

I know what to do with it.
In my garden I sit where
The windows are open.
The tanager sings.
I do not see him,
A fear of mankind
And a modest glory
Surround him.
They say the gods don't come down here.
I wait in the sun
Not despairing
And the breath of happiness
Brushes my sleeve.

The Remarkable Heavens

For Ron Smith

We are all sailing in a circle,
The globe leans toward the seasons.
We are a part of heavenly declensions
Doing what we have to do, ice
And icy icebergs or, inclined
The other way, steamy swamps,
The damp crocodile in them,
O tears. What shall we do
Taken for a ride around the sky?
Stars blink in the passage, the sun
Goes up and down while the hermit prays.
Yesterday we passed through Leo,
The zodiac a ninth month gone and
No parturition. Last
Monday fortnight I observed
The moon at the lake-edge with my love.
It was only half there. Tomorrow
I master astronomy and play like Liszt.
I can remember sirens I cranked
Going round corners, fires dreamed;
Cabooses rode. Now I take up
Heaven. Orion went out just now
Quenched by a horizon and the pole star
Just swung around and stayed there.

April

The tilting of the earth continuing
Flowers will come up, the sun
Has been out now for nine hours.
New movements following runnels
Down slants between pebbles
Can be remarked by their sparkle;
Motion of air makes puddles
Known. Pale shoots all
Month out of the sun are ready;
The heart aches with the shortness of life.
Patches of soil appear and the lid
Of the bin lies off from the trash
Collector. The end of the violence of the world
Is awaited. Nations hold back.
Young men want their love enfolded;
Fern fronds are furled tight.
Watchers acknowledge the worth of worship.

April, Again

Come on now, I told myself,
Consider wholly love, love
While the sun, after days,
Is out and there is a little joy
In the world between harsh sorrow.
There, again, the sun is out.
Snow spreads aside and April
Is under foot. It is the time,
The time eyes know that grass
Comes under north slopes
And the world is wide on condition
The people in it are widely
Overlooked and what they do
And the heart is willing to concede
Something is about to happen
Like the complicated simplicity
Of blossom and the movement of wings.
Day is able to include even her.
Her movements and practicalities and loving.
Death hasn't yet stepped in.
It's joy, partly, and the heart is voluble
In the way first mentioned above.
On the earth sun is come.

Brief for Helios

He ought to have been top banana.
They had him driving chariots back and forth
All weathers while Zeus ran around screwing cows,
Hurling thunderbolts every direction
At mortals half his size. He spilled the beans
To sooty Hephaestus about Aphrodite in bed
With War, dumb guy. The whole of Athens
Was appalled when Anaxagoras declared him
A burning cinder. We of course agree.
But don't get too Canadian; strip him
Of celestial presence, chariot, charm and axle,
He's still up and around. Toads love him
Squat on their swampy bottoms, we do,
Lizards shift their dun to gold,
Females do, their long lithy limbs,
Jars and bottles beside them. Who doesn't?
Don't get the idea he's over,
Urging springtime in and out of season,
Getting muddy seeds uptight.
Whole cities exit, Helios out.

Allhallows Eve

Until the dust from the broom came
In the beam from the basement window
The suncast was invisible. It squared
Tangled. The smash on the far wall
Hit cement low down since the sun
Stood high over the next house
And the elm at the roadway. Crammed
With dancing dust, anywhere near it
Man sneezed.

        The ladder was put
Away, halloween was on
The doorstep, the second day All Souls.
Lucifer! he shouldn't have fallen to Satan.
The beam was glorious, dust in it,
Autumn leaves were raked and the bulbs
In, the gates to Eden open,
No one needed to climb walls.

Disproportion

Chalk this up: never before
Has such praise been given
Snow on the limbs of trees shaken
In a shoddy wind,
Have sparks exploded
In a stardom of glory
Thus from logs...
Two instances will do
Of the prodigiousness
As I sit here,
The window on my left on winter,
The fire on my right
Burning where the fireplace is.

     Sprawl banners,
Slogans raise to the turn of events,
Psalteries and song even,
To all sorts,
To the procedures of
Being here, to knowledge of
Progressions, to imposed goings even.
The snow falls,
The fire burns.
I engage prodigies.

The Bronze Doors at Pisa

Taller than two monks, the bronze doors at Pisa,
In one oblong the angel of the Lord on Jesus' sepulchre
Swinging his feet. Hammerwork
Sophisticated with innocence
More in love with heaven than chapels of rococo
Florid with space.
Lord, deliver us!
Anonymity, simpleness and faith.

Who Began It and What For

O this search for the celestial possible
Is a hoo hoo hoo. Who indeed,
God on his fluff or where the beetle crawls,
Bearer of death, to solve it all
Where all is pall. Scarabs scamper.
Hoo indeed, *philosophe*,
Turning the clock around.

   The lark's on the wing where the moon
Is up to her gilded tricks.

   Blessed be the sun and the conundrum
Of God if this day last and we are not
Shovelled under. Blessed be Who
Who lists as he lists sending us toward divinity!
What dig except it be
The celestial worm on the illimitable hook?

Sermon on Accumulation, A Brief One

Growth, not accretion. Quantity
Is the fever of the times—the gross
Product; accumulations swamp
The mind, God and Gallup, Pericles
And Marx, may the noisy podium
Find distinction. Number nothing
Except by the heart. Who falls in love with people?
Love is singular.
The earthworm for his antics,
Dolphins for their song, each of us
For love, ears stopped to the sum
The mythy sirens prove, Odysseus
On his periplum ten years home
To true Penelope who spun.
Learned scholars doubt if Adam could add.

Lamp-Bulb for the Corner

That myths about can have light,
The man in the Hydro's hoist bucket
Replaces the burnt-out bulb
In the bracket on the telephone pole
At the top of the hill beside the lake,
The bulb dead for weeks so that Venus
Up over the winter equinox
Like a dazzling chip of diamond never
Shone so brazenly, Helen
On her fur rug waiting for Paris
Never as dazzling to the boob.
Methodists in the dark veer off
From the amorous corner knowing nightly
Doings too good to be good.
So, Troilus in his cloak in darkest
Troy, Criseyde waiting nude
Wanting to be naked to the town.
Alas for burnt-out love.
Joists heft gingerly him
With the brand-new bulb, the hot
Line to the toasters in the next
Houses just skipping his shoulder.
Up under, he knocks snow,
His sleeve catching the fall so
He dances in his damned red bucket.
Contact's twisted into. Jaundiced
Search-beam blinks round,
The world well lost. The globe
Is screwed. Cocks crow, comings
Slippery with glow. The buff truck's
Bluff joints clamp down,
Hard hat collapsed in his bucket-
truck goes, circuits renewed.

At the Ca' Pesaro

Music, modest as in this palazzo,
At the piano here, the Ca' Pesaro,
Canal Grande. And in how many places...
Madame's handkerchief before she plays,
Seta pura the low-cut gown
As thought of as the music, Brahms,
Berg and his nerve-ends; rubbish
In the canal, rinds, zucchini tops,
Yesterday's soaked news floating
Where Byron swam and Browning loved.
Out through the windows *Intermezzo*
For the passing world, Brahms imbibing
His coffee, Madame rendering, impervious
To the *vaporetto*'s thump.

Garden Information on Behalf of Hummingbirds

Red trumpet-shaped flowers,
Not only to match the long tongues
But to lessen competition of bees,
And red since hummingbirds
See blue less well. Energy
Burnt at such a rate, ruby
Throats must hibernate at night.

This for those who love them. More:
They hover, therefore plant blossoms
Accordingly, pendulous fuchsias
For instance, rich in nectar, without
The landing platforms bee-flowers
Have, winter mint is good,
Jewelweed and spiderflower.

They love to sip in sunshine beebalm
And columbine, coralbells
And *phlox divaricata* for those
With latin. Fragrance or lack of it
Is of no consequence. Among the vines
And shrubs, the scarlet runner bean
Is fine, beautybush and lilacs.

All this for a flash of colour hardly.
Preferably include a wall which
In itself can be attractive and occupies
Little space while holding up flowers.
A succession of blossoms up to the last
Of August is to be thought of, then
The birds head south. Frost threatens.

Dirge for Gardens

That robin running around the new-mown
Lawn listening for worms, I worked hard for.
The skin at the fork of my thumb and forefinger's
Gone shoving the machine. I straighten a bent-over
Pansy, alert at the whistle in my ear.
Redstarts are about. A wasp goes into the hole
In the paper-grey cone stuck under the angle
Of the kitchen-door projection of roof.
But they don't take advantage, the birds and wasps.
It's the labour for the worm bothers me—'mown grass'
Say the psalms of David, the old testy monk.
What's it for has a way of getting into the best
Of labour, though I suppose ambition is worthy of its
                                                    abrasions.
The robin has given up pulling worms,
Putting labour doubly in question...

The Stars Settled

She opened the door wide to the verandah,
"Hello world! How are you doing?"
I've heard her say that a hundred times,
Each time earth consolidates,
Stars settle and my heart grabs
Ahold. Everything works. Syria
Loves Israel, a short circuit
Of the refrigerator is nothing, the whole
Of winter hails spring, and frogs
Boom from moonlit trees. Yes.
"Hello world" and I am translated
And doomsday somebody else's concern.

1981

CONFLICTS OF SPRING

The desire to be at the end of distances.
—WALLACE STEVENS

The Sun in the Garden

I

Wallace Stevens is wrong: he says,
"A poem need not have a meaning
And like most things in nature
Often does not have." He is slipshod.
He was in the insurance business,
He ought to have known better.

I examine this slug that has crawled up
Into the saucer of my cup of tea.
It has two protrusions out of its head
And apparently absorbs food
Through its foot's peristalsis:
Repugnance after my sugar.

Also after the roses. The garden
Looks like it. The protuberances
Move out almost imperceptibly
But it doesn't fool what it senses
Or me. Beauty is taken in,
Blind repugnance or not. It squashes.

I snip it with my fingers off
The saucer, enough of it had. I walk
The rest of the day in the garden knowing
Something is futile. I have meaning.
I have to counteract it. I look up
Evolution, religion, love.

II

What gave matter its propensities
Agitates me. I want the answer,
Dying to get it is no answer,
I'm here now with circumstance,
Not exalted with God. I sit in the sun
And think of astrophysics. I am
Not too far and not too near
The sun, gravity is at work and the pitch
Off the centre into space
Equated with pull; the earth rounds,
Grass grows, sperm is kept warm,
Man, not yet having punctured
Van Allen's Belt, no shrunken ort;
Great enough the fire to reach
From sun to where I sit downed
By reasons why. There it burns,
The radioactive hunk, just
Far enough: the heart lifts up;
Men are reluctant to go to war
Until the harvest's in.

                    Cynicism.
Why not, heaven under wraps
And mankind dying to get it?

Swept up into Light (to use the word
That doesn't dogmatize) such death,
Such suction into the Absolute,
Is rip-off, counterfeit, wormy hook.
Currency while the grass is green
And sun a personal insult not
To ascribe it, is the only downright coin.
There it shines. Here I am.

IV

Faith's not enough. To probables with faith!
Perception is the satisfaction.
There is a mountain stream I put
My hand in, the rush of slanted water
Laves the fist and wrist around,
The extremest sense in the world
So cold I yank my hand out
Before I become God. That's
The only handout, not faith:
Knowledge so if I go back
To the mountain stream I can trust
Cold.

    I add it up: have
Heaven and convict the moment;
Now levels with everyone.

The concrete stream and why the cosmos
Is ordered (insatiable tall order):
Then I'll shrug here in the sun
Warm enough for love and the impatiens
Flower red down the garden path.

The Arrival of Wisdom

Of course the truth is there's no design,
Just process: which settles all-seeing God for good
And Him as a chemist mixing combinations
To get what He could declare without it,
Wanting to be worshipped, pitching beginnings
With a Bang into teleological void.

Truth goes on solving nothing, gluons
And quarks combine, come apart, unmindful, stars
Go out, suns come on, the clutter ever
Expanding; sheep on the meadow chew, chew,
Man makes mince, until his neck-thongs shrivel
And breath departs lugging its baggage
Of unaccomplished dreams. What a celestial
Tautology to get there! fun in the dreaming,
Irony in choice, tragedy in the waste,
Getting nowhere with injustice.

Faith is an ignorance. Love without hurt
The only choice.

Conflicts of Spring

After the autumn burns down again
The earth will turn cold until
Spring's opulence. The defection of summer
Is assured and the turning of autumn
Is assured. Repeated with frozen branches
Who will believe in spring's beginning?
It is hard, it is a hard act to follow,
These terminations of blossoms.
Even if the time come of affirmation
It is for others, never permanent
In the slipshod heart;
That will stop.
Trees are green for us only for a time
No matter how they go on
For whatever proclamations of indifference,
Hullaballoo.
The phony clown gets it
However he beats his drum.
Love falls out of love; spring,
A subject in the academies.

The Colour of the Crystal Day

Burnished silver is the colour of
The still calm winter day.
Spread snow from last night
Lies along the fir branches
Dark beaten green in survival.
The fall was light, only a token
Whiteness of what has gone before
But no less beautiful in crystal freezings
That last a moment held in air,
Symmetry extricable on dark sleeves
Held out. And sorrows still the same:
The man of speech holding out
Wordless his son starved;
Nearer home, she who died
Yesterday. Elegies are constant—
Burnished silver or not, the sky
Of winter. The unanswerable moment
Comes, love denied or had,
This love a condition of being here
As this day still calm, no turmoil
Except what's been or is to be:
The winter crystal silver light,
The unaccounted-for denial of love.

Segment of Ten Minutes

Never having clasped life so tightly
As in the leaving of it, I listen to the call
Of birds as though trees were an ultimate purpose.
I sit in the sun and grieve on behalf of ancestors,
I get up and put water on the boil for something,
I watch tap water in envy,
This a.m., changing water
In vases of flowers to keep colour
Going I put my mouth in the depths
Of a peony and said *Love*.

                I am daft.
This adulation I must stop.
Watching mankind makes it easy,
The sham, the gather and sanctification,
Of cheapness, the handwashing; having enough
Is easy enough—to have done and get out of it.
But not these presents, the standing in sun,
The more than possibility of loving her,
This morning's vastly responsible announcements,
Bats, belfry, proclamations,
Bees at blossoms—the whole nightshirt
Get-up and celestial existence of existence.
Sun just reached the scarlet geranium
Set out in the antique fire-bucket.

Attached Here With Birthdays

Micturition and dawns, not one
Without the other, current for life.
Amalgam of rude civilities!
Not a naked early riser
Isn't in for it, handsomeness
In contempt, aspirations
In contradiction. Coming and becoming
Spin round the world: Tekakwitha,
Hooks in her flesh absolving sin
While loveliness lies in the sun and tans
Her joy. Mortalities of toilet!
Wheelchair, swaddling, whatever drinks
Has to go, nothing's for it.
Epitaphs prove the worth of repairs,
Birthdays confirm the ending. Innocence
Plucks the paradox: Noah pounds
His planks, flagellants mock their maker.

Still we wouldn't be without it,
Take-offs, aftermaths and plumbing.
Notice at brink of dawn what's up!
Lovers love it, popes start washing...

Creation Simplified

God and the earth too,
Neither possible without
The other, the one exclusive,

Done for, lacking the other,
God writing *a*
Capella for the angels

While we alarmed yank
Changes in the steeple.
God contemplated,

Thought it out ... liking
The heavenly look of it, committed
Himself to earthenware:

No son without the father,
The holy ghost like a dove
Hovering over the funeral.

Stanzas to Little Jack Horner

What questions to be asked of the here
And now, eh? Sackcloths and ashes,
Monks in cloisters, whole families saved.

Alas that he should miss heaven
For being little Jack Horner,
His pie in his lap with good purple

Suckable plums. He is cornered, painted
In, his brush crimson and dipped
In cans, abilities of green.

Was he wrong? Tarzan was his reading
And not Jonah under a wilting gourd.
He girded his loins, swung trees.

His immediate preference not celestial,
But sundowns and prairies, pioneers
Turning cartwheels to the next corral.

Among the Wheatfields

The sky had amplitude, so had the great fields.
I had difficulty in claiming the sky so wide was
The horizon. So windswept was the grass
I stood there, a probable of contemplation
In the wideness of eternity. My heart was small, it is four
Inches across, but I knew the directions found there,
I knew in its compass was all I needed to know
Of width, of limits farthest from supposition:
The progress of wind in the stalks, the wheatspears
Rust-colour, the rasp of a particular love.
I awaited the final knowledge of knowing,
The consolidation of eternity; yet what I knew,
The place where I was wholly, was already what
Those absolutes are. The trouble of final
Exaltation, this fieldwork finished with,
The going, was still given over to that which I would
Not have: completion, joy without desire,
The whole field done with that is joyful death.

A Slight Wind and White Flowers

The slightest wind moved the white wave
Of saxifrage—the five-petal flower
That tumbles stone walls, destruction that likes
Spring. A bee clung and swung a stem of it,
The wind not the only mover, teeming
Propagation was also,
Thigh-carried pollen. The sequence
Only needed death in it
To complete all topics possible
To be thought of. But death wasn't
In it this time, the afternoon
Was too forgetful, sun on rockfoil,
The bee at work, termination something
That could take care of itself. Small
Wars were on elsewhere but here were acts
Without man in them—except that someone
Has to be around to make the act of perceiving.
Luck had it that ambition wasn't around,
Only life teeming and a day for it,
Not to die in but to accomplish
Divine events, acrobatics on stems,
A slight wind and white flowers.

Snow, White Birches, Bach

"The music is older the second time
The repeat is played and so should have
The experience behind it of the statement made"—
Thus Harold Samuel of playing Bach.
And this brevity of sun is not
The same. Briefer, briefer. Yet now
More glorious for all its going down.

The lesson's learned, the brilliant snow
Is yesterday's when we could not stand
Its going, knowing less of possession
And wanting what a thousand blazings
Could give us—even as these trees,
White birches slanting a forest's
Darkness with their tallest sanctions,
A crossing that we could not have
Without their bending—

                   Now, the repeat,
All that warning behind it,
Is its purpose, acceptance got to.
The sun on snow, white birch,
These hills and lake, as experienced
Music is, are culmination,
The hour, acknowledgement alone.

The Shuttered Dawn

The great man comes to his finish ninety
Times, capable of nothing more,
Sunset is as the sunset that
First day: tomorrows, accomplished
As much as can be hazarded on one throw,
The farthest possibilities read
On lens and slide. I think of Gaudier
Killed on the front in '17
The future of sculpture carved in the wood
Of the rifle-butt, all he had
Before the shrapnel closed his throat;
Titian, for ninety years each portrait
His last. Born to greatness is the man
Who sees his skull:

            Again that pool
Is come to that the torrent splashed to rainbow—
That love is made whose finish was all
That there was though morning was at the shutter
Stars that night would be held by.

March is a Muddy Month

I   *The Woods, Still Winter*

The snow in the far woods falling, he bends
Down to remove the snow from his mukluks,
Looking around him gazing at the falling
Snow, wondering at the continual fall,
Thinking of the fire burning, the place
He loves over all places but loving
The clearing, the white birch (again)
Slanting the firs heavy with fresh
Burden, the continual snow falling.
He thinks of the impossibility perhaps
Of coming tomorrow. The woods need
The man in it somewhere; concern.
With his finger he takes the white rim
Of snow away from his boots, looks up
At the winter a moment; moves on.

II   *Delays of Spring*

The earth inclines, dusk comes later
Than supposed. The long snow
Steadies from the lack of sun,
Lucent as crystal, the light
Held in still. All night
Is heard the rushing stream, then
No more. It is colder, holding
Is everywhere, lagging drifts
Stay. On hills darkening
No word comes of meltings.

This will not last. Deep as the frost
Is, the dirty scaffoldings,
The crusted snow will crumble, waters will rush
In places thrown over
And there will be openings.
People will be careful of the world who
Have learned to get through winter.

III *March Assumed*

The sun is still high.
All morning a sift of snow
And cloud; and yet,there,
Hazed gold changing
Golden now that noon
Is passed. A molten gold.
Southward from this window,
Behind the elm black
Against the haze, its complex
Of black branches sifted
With white, the sun's announcements.
The weather will clear, roads will be
Passable, on the lake-ice
Men fishing. Existence
Will happen and

No notice taken,
Desolation assumed;
At the grandstand sun,
Not a fanfare,
Not a brass tilted.
Nothing announces nothing.
Plenty, a hole in the ice.
The nag Pegasus, wings
On, gone in the bellows.
Sad raspings. A complex
Of valuables, a paraphernalia
Of mint coinage, the sun up,
Not believed in.

IV *Halfway Through March*

This is the time of seeds,
For the edges of red shoots
Under leaves, for open
Snowdrops though. Evidence of spring.
Patches of snow hold out
On the banks lying north
Where the drift was thickest.
The curling rink
Holds a sugaring off.

The bed is made
With the fresh sheets,
The window is open,
The double one pushed back
On its crooked side brackets.
The noise of the rush of meltwater
Pours down the steep roadway
Where it shouldn't run,
The culvert still frozen solid.

I try to adjust what is known
To new announcements.
The rage isn't easy.
Small minds persuade their triumph,
The electrode harms
Where no mark is left,
Abraham puts the knife
Through the throat of Isaac.
Channels run littleness.

Afternoon

The jet bores the blue. Drives in.
The military are practising security,
Training summer. There's a chill in the air.
Every once in a while a narrow breeze
Comes in, just a gentle sideswipe,
Over the hedge and then past the lone aster.
The hummingbird has gone south.
Though there is a blue sail on the lake,
A blue candystick canvas
Going this way and then that
Catching the chill breeze,
Though not all summer employment
Has gone,
The plane is up there seeking assurance,
A civilized man and his grandson
Have just been blown up in their boat
In the grand scene of Sligo,
The Irish love violence.
A terrible beauty is born.
        Why there should be
Sadness
Over the garden
Is not immediately apparent,
Someone away for the earlier months perhaps
Who owned the garden.
Gardens ask attention.
When the sun went in
In that loud heaven,
Summer intimations,
Civilities, were over.

Thoughts on a Narrow Night

It would seem that God is in nature
But not in history. Roses bloom
And are pretty. We can smell them. We also
Smell ovens if you know what I mean.
Last year was difficult for the roses,
The soil impoverished, knowledge to enrich it
Properly was lacking, the earth too
Clay to begin with. Anyhow, despite
Last year and the culture, flowers
Do bloom. So God's in His heaven.
No sarcasm meant. We all
Appreciate the life force
That drives the universe, stallions,
Jesuit, Napoleon and other ambitions
Mentionable which can be laid claim to.
No offence:
God gives the food, we cook it.
It's the lack of divine
Intervention that's unaccountable.
Loaves and fishes. But divinity since then?
Best leave contemplation of history out of it
And go smell jonquils.

Outburst for February

The archaic Greeks carved smiling naked man;
Michelangelo cut stone;
Beethoven,
So the story goes,
Poured soup
Over the talker's head.

Now fools praise self-portraits.

To the solitary mountains! the pools!
Whatever fresh cold lake water there is to dive into...

Incident out of Southeast Asia

They crucify youth in Cambodia,
However not with nails, just rope
From the wrists to the crosspiece, the belly
Pulled up and out pretty much
But easier than Jesus had it, the pull
On the joints less, the balls of his feet
Being on the ground. The boy
Stole some rice.
Jesus stole more.
He will be cut down eventually.
None the worse except for the redemption.

124

In the Night

Out of the throat of night
Comes the cry,
Long and in anguish.
The hackles of my head
Raise, I raise my head...
Against the thermal windows
Across the winter
Comes the cry.
Man's cry.
As if in agony.

When the Light of the Last Star
is Extinguished

There it is: a recognition
Of ourselves or that final
Shudder as the stars go out.

Six Impromptus

I   On Beginnings

What made the markings on the sandpiper
Camouflage him so well you can't
See a chick at three feet?
The birdbrain didn't take thought
About it, the grey and bluff in patches
That mark the tundra. Genes? How could
They match the landscape, a billion years
Of snuggling into climates, the calamus
Shooting warnings up its quill
Until the vane shot ruffled colour
Through its terror compounded into
Crazy permanence? Look at the victim
Spread his wings, give his piping
Call, free of the predator's luck
And fly to God. Ah, God did it.
Worked out the pattern over the years
To fool His chicken lovers, loving
Birds? Yes, maybe, but I doubt
The evolutionary bit—
So much easier declaring facts
Once and for all. Creation has time;
Still, why evolve? Perhaps God's becoming
Too, gills turning into
His tonsils, so to speak? But that
Sounds doubtful considering the instant
Thought which foresaw it all.
Triply puzzling, this ticklish question
Of feathers when you put them alongside
Iron both falling in a vacuum.

II *On Miracles*

How mankind has managed to come this far
Is anybody's guess. Think of the length
Man's loved man, exclaiming benefits,
Morals, Marx, and grace through profit.
The gentle jackal isn't in it.
How we got here is insoluble.
We should have been a bloody footprint
In Africa.

Free choice alone gives man dignity.
So God had to create evil.
Why the fuss and bother about it,
Evil's existence? The shark slips,
The lion tears the gazelle apart,
Man is in the midst of confusion,
The flesh wants and the brainless blow
Jesus' legs off. Choosing
Makes all the difference, His lovely body
Taken on, we get to dignity.
And then there is Adam less the apple,
Fat around his middle saying
Prayers by rote. Judas had
A choice, poor solitary guy, but Destiny,
Unattractive as ever, had
A hand in it and got him hung.
How get Jesus to hang properly
Otherwise? You have to have
Fate sometimes, man persists
Too much. The choice left open
Makes us consider the harder course is
The goal to make. Think if Jesus
Let the world go hang, Voltaire
Stuck to gardening, Churchill
Had flinched, Falstaff took a cup
Of senna tea of a morning?
Oh no, choice explains
The dignifying, evil shunned.

I planted Athena, owl, on the book
That wouldn't stay open, weighty enough
To hold down the pages—the owl
A paperweight done in enamelled
White, red, and yellow with two
Green eyes bought at a shop in the Plaka
Plato once walked by on his way
To listen to Socrates spout, the young
Men jumping around, their cocks
Bouncing which pleased the old man
Who had Hermes in his garden and hemlock
On his cupboard shelf... Wisdom
To hold down poetry (the thick book
Was poems). How sexy owls became
The emblem of Athena who isn't remains
Greek, it certainly was topheavy
When placed in conjunction with poetry which gets
Its purchase lower down on that
Which men die for, not her
Standing up there in the Parthenon
In greaves and helmet, clothed in the peplos
No doubt cotton like the hose
Worn by those brisk girls on bicycles
At Oxford... I retreat back down the hill
To the gymnasium where Plato picks
His teeth watching athletes...

                        The book
Just sprang back on its spine, *zap*,
Athena's owl shot from its perch...

v   *On Trivial Things*

Three times I fed the birds—not thinking
Much of Peter with his bird and its thrice
Crowing *Watch Out* for the charity of the Lord—
More of my father putting his hand in his trouser
Pocket when he didn't have much but knowing
The movie serial at the Premier Theatre read:
Come Next Week, and I got the dime to go—
A deed as divine though with less theology in it
Than Peter and the crowing hard as a rock.
Remembering that how the next chapter came out
Meant the world and applying that to seeds,
I poured them out at three dollars a bag
And spread them on the board (the *bed* was provided
Free of charge by the bird-loving Lord)—
The wood board across the corner of the verandah
Railings set up to supply a needed winter
Grace—the grosbeaks fighting for possession,
The redpolls learning from them to be nasty,
Ready to feint flight because of their size,
Cracking husks like mad, thrashing air,
The board too narrow to hold them all,
Clearing the plank clean then waiting in the trees.
All is greed, everything is greed—
After the first necessity. I went back down
To the cellar and got more expensive seed.
Silly how the trivial is the world.
Three times I spread the food, not really
Thinking of remorseful Peter denying Somebody
But of my father, myself at the Premier Theatre
Wondering how Antonio Moreno, the hero,
Would get out of the pit the villain put him in,
The boulder above, the lantern burning the rope
That held it, in "The Perils of Thunder Mountain."

VI   *On Profusion*

Not one but a ramble of flowers
Is necessary, a single bloom
Graces a shelf but when was Eden
Not a garden and Adam digging?
The nerves want profusion, a license
Of you know what, smell and blossom,
Worm and sunslap all over the place.
Not less than extravagance will do.
Perfection's parsimonious, only
The profligate flaw will do—to perfect
The poet in us. Jewels in the mud.
Nine Symphonies and Haydn's you don't
Know how many which from which.
Moiseiwitsch put the text in its place,
Sprezzatura was what he was after,
Tempo rubato, missed notes
All over the place under the piano,
But what a recital, wot a recital!
Bach never stopped playing
Morning, noon and night on his organ
(Ahem...). God is in the profusion
Business, what with His push-ups
And prohibitions. Words, words,
Joyce was after; three floorsful
Picasso painted his fraudulent facts.
May there be not one
But a thousand boiled lobsters fresh
From the tank for the menus of hopeless lovers.

Letter to Akhenaten

You put by the loveliest woman in Egypt
To take up with your brother. You thought
Love was all one and truth so potent
You could make it public. Nefertiti
Went to the North Palace and Smenkhara
The golden boy was surrogate for your own
Ugliness. Misfortune all round. The Window
Of Appearances at which you made everyone
Stand naked in truth before the populace,
Didn't work. The viewers were curious or shocked,
The truth wasn't what should be achieved.
Illusion was, the pun on habit clothed.
Not pot-bellies but rainbows and panoply.
You tried it with God, making Him one,
The one Aten, not cow-eared Hathor,
Horus the night-hawk and Khons with a boat
And moonshine. It was no good, monotheism.
The temple wants diversity, more money in it,
Your sundisk with its rays of little hands
Giving breath to the nostrils, your shining Light,
Wasn't enough though you move a city .
Down the Nile. The old alleys are what
Men want, familiar establishments. You know
Where you stand then, not some
Abstract Benevolence up over the horizon
Somewhere. Cover your belly, go back toThebes,
Give up believing your truth is my truth.
Truth is what is convenient and comfortable.
You can't win the world over with poetry.

Rondo in Triads

1

History marks the line on
The palm of my hand the way
I go.

2

The long slender bone with
The manacle on it is my
Right arm.

3

And in my eyes is the sight
Of the soft bruise from
The gunbutt.

4

I sit in my chair and the arch
Of my ankle is split
By the spike.

5

I watch the man running with his child
From the bomb. I intend to go out to help
Them.

6

I mistake the stars of heaven
As I choose between my right hand
And my other.

7

Whole cities abuse God for
The manner of their choice. Persia
And Rome.

8
Scarlatti, famous for crossing hands,
Became so fat he was unable to play
In this position.

9
O I could cry out with beauty
Of hills, the poem's tension that is
My love.

10
"The sex member has a poetic power
Like a meteor," says Miro. I looked
At the heavens.

11
"The simplest things give me ideas," he says,
Walking across his unmarked canvas
In dirty shoes.

12
The slanted plaster ceiling of the attic
Had cracks in it Michelangelo
Made use of.

13
The keyboard, recall, got that width
Because ladies in hoopskirts loved
To play duets.

14
They say Mozart crossed the Alps
Without once looking up from the scores
On his lap.

15

Cézanne's apples. Who cares whether
They are sweet or sour? I love
Appleness.

16

An investigating spectroscope
Declares flowers are naturally blind
To green.

17

Fap. I listen to beavers. *Fap.*
Hunt a bird who has to learn
To build a nest.

18

I walk with my love in the wide world.
Comets burst and pincers close
Around a moth.

19

And the earth is indifferent to the diamond in it.
"Oh, mes amis, j'ai nostalgie de la boue!"
Cried Rachel.

20

Along my coatsleeve the fire
Of thought. In my mouth the taste
Of words.

Singular Love Poem

—*Singularity: the density from which the cosmos re-begins.*

It was a singularity,
The possibility that love
Should be as it is.

Stars fled density,
Constellations sought
Their areas, an astonishment

Of places ruled
The night, purposes were evident
That had not been known before.

Coruscations of spirals
Gathered galaxies, suns
Shone in unusual stations.

It was hard not to move
Toward exaggeration yet the farthest
Interpretations were valid,

I was convinced beyond all errors.
I looked at the immediacy,
The heavens as rejoicings.

Epic Quit at the First Stanza

I have sat on the great gate-stone
At Tiryns where Jason came
And Heracles ruled.

It was with my love though; not Argo
And the gold fleece, Mycenae itself,
Counted; whether

The gate-lintel was royal entrance
Or latch-door to outside meadow
Less than the walk

On the dusty road back toward Nafplion
Where we came, wandered and shopped
For woven mats

Made as maidens made them before
Troy fell. Myths less than
Our knowing them.

All the sun trembled in the bay below.
A milkgoat cropped the roadside
Where we sat,

The rattled bus an hour late,
The sun on our shoulders where Tiryns crumbled
And crickets sang.

Explanation Using Some
Domestic Parallels

Unlike the noisy cricket
Deaf to its own song,
The poet singly listens
To the sawing of
His own hind legs.

The irreplaceable reconstitution
Of desirable experience
Is what he scrapes out but not
The only thing
He euphorically means.

The kettle of fish would boil over
With clarity so to speak,
Taps in midst of heatwaves
Run breathless
Spring water,

Heaven would put pleas on its backburners
And buckets of risen bread,
That yeast in them, go bust
Overflowing
If the world

Listened. Listen to him go on
Sawing one leg on the other
Too sane to be crazy
But crazy as a hope
To keep on scraping.

Twelfth-Century Music

Where the cathedral yard holds regals,
Tambourine shivers and shawms take cold.
The mason puts his tools away,
His truth-telling chisel and his gospel
Square; listens. The carpenter climbs
Down his ladder and the glazier from
His crosshatch scaffold; his head shakes
At what the carver has done, the abbot
Crosseyed with his tongue raspberried
On a corbel. They hark to the rebec and the drum
Beating out contagious measure.

O the great joy as the house
Of the Virgin is blessèd built up!
The noise and O the nooks and niches
Of the saints standing near the elegies
Of glazed glass leaded in!
What praying and incompletion!

                              The far
Fields stretch away to the linns.

Around and around, girl and boy
Bow and dance to the nasaling music.
The prebendary looks on stingily.

What warmth to the soul! Clotilde is shy.
O the Round of the Incarnation!

GRADATIONS OF GRANDEUR

The essential thing in a poet
is that he builds us his world.
—EZRA POUND

Gradations of Grandeur

1   *The world is worth living.*

Gradations of grandeur descend
And all is reality, sitting here
In the sun, the mind's integrations

Proof, accumulations ply on ply
Real as diamonds dug. We carry
With us assortments to fulfil ourselves

If not high heaven, the will triumphant
At least as far as death, the trouble
Worth it if at most no further.

Mighty solaces inhere, ahead of,
Beyond disintegration of eyes
And limbs; marring of the handsome

Body no disproof the stuff
Of nostrils being ceased. The wave
Is motion through it, not ocean carted

Here to there. So the exact
Crystal keeps its tang, the sculptured
Bronze doors of Novgorod

Are a continuity, what
We have, paradigm clear
In the mind, buildings, music made,

The hoofed green jade horse
Striding the graves of old China,
Upon the stage, Justice Shallow's

Chimes at midnight—for a moment,
Little of it perhaps, it's possible, probable,
Nothing but a brief hiatus.

The intuitive persists. Men
Die in catacombs engraving
Crosses, she in scarcity feeds

A child so he can get to obstinate
Heaven. Man is cranky on
The subject, Galileo mutters

Nonetheless it moves, his proof
Jupiter's four moons in his pocket.
Cranmer burns his pen hand first

That signed the recantation, Thomas
Contributes his head. Heaven or mud,
There's proof enough, grandeur is had.

Violence is sick for it, killing
Man to get on camera, punks,
As popes, on knees probationary

For heaven. To think about it's worth it.
That's a thrush that sings, figure
Hidden in the growth of leaves.

2   *Man is unreliable.*

What man makes of it often
Is death, more often than
We care to think of. Auschwitz's

Smell; the bulldozer brought up,
The dead too much for carting;
Anyway, the load too much.

144

Stupidity can be overcome.

Stupidity's term can be revulsion.
It depends. On angels descending,
Our own fingers' scorched pain.

Gradations of goodness add up and
Stupidity gets it. Occasionally.
Pulled from corpses, gold teeth

Convey more than dentistry. Sometimes.
The creative mind uses suffering.
Jesus hung on some heavenly nails.

Nonetheless... would He had had
Magdalene in bed, a grand
Son for Mary. But no one then

Would believe the sheets divine, not shrouds,
We like our porridge mixed with Lent,
Penitential endings. Was there

Ever a non-sour religion,
No crepe in it, Jahveh
Holding His sides, Buddha bent

Double? Still, something wishes
Better... Quasimodo ringing
Bells, Salem done with dunking.

Man is devious though.

We have got as far as tin cups
For the hopeless, malice spared
Those with cancer. We realize

No one is perfect, especially the better
Than ourselves when things aren't
So good for them. We feel better.

Still, there's hope.

Inconceivable heaven we hold
Inalienable. Forget the obscurantists
Of the world for a moment, they deal

With themselves badly, eventually.
The wind in that tree is scintillant sun
The whole of heaven blue behind it.

Coition's daredown doter makes
Joy, women glad of sons.
That's natural. So is love.

Try to prohibit it and see.
The better runs the world, Curie
Singed, Anne concealed, grandeur

Done. Nothing has destroyed us we
Would hold dear. We admit
Falsity but hold love dear.

6   *There's a margin for joy.*

Flowers grow without legalities.
What have the bending hills to do
With briefs, November's prosecution?

So far, good air's free
For the lungs without cessation pending
Legislation. Still is there margin

For joy. We breathe still, drenched
By the comber we climbed out of,
Wow, plunged into air, cleanly

Regale ourselves with mountains zipped
By a bracing wind, compound solace
With a sunrise, breath big.

Let alone, grass grows.
Intricacy flounders, out fishing.
Plato cures his whereabouts sneezing.

Her song was memorable, offkey singing
In the garden. So, the poem,
The whole line unasked given.

7   *Intuition is durable.*

Being impels, compels the blood
Circling in ignorance, chemicals
Combusted by high heaven blue

And serene, the poem knowing, the hand
That writes it with about as much
Knowledge of perfection as a lover

At it. Who stops, grooms
His lips for a minute, reads the clock,
To consider the teleology of her?

We grab the morning stars or none,
The credit for it and shut up.
Heaven winks or winces or wins.

8   *Being is positive.*

Philosophies sit around tables
Disposing thumbs and crumbs and condoms.
Wham comes heaven and solves the nonce.

9 *The sun rises.*

The man of jowls suddenly gets up
And stretches; Jeremiah feels
Good. In the gloom sun comes

Where owls defile sarcophagi.
Men work misliking stars.
Misanthropy becomes beet crops.

Angels come down and get into it,
Out of modesty in worn jeans.
That is to say, it sometimes works.

10 *Assertions assort the world.*

"Of this image and love, I compose
Myself of these." Whether it be
A woman mixing cake with added

Dollops, batter or matter, or she
Of the cruse anointing Jesus' feet.
His sex stirred. How couldn't it?

In need of oil, ingenuity
Brought epical pipelines down from Alaska,
Works of great consequence, logistics

Considering the feelings of migrating moose.
This one contemplated a symphony.
Dreams compel, sort the world,

The upshot sprung as though from nowhere.
The wind once sat in an odd
Quarter yet the orange sail

On the lake's blue ten years later
Thought of, quieted his heart.
Dame Clara Butt's high C

Cracked a glass. It took five
Men to carry Catherine's train,
What we would comes after us.

11   *Not all is guesswork.*

What conclusions we can reach
Because of guess, knowing no better,
Is Beethoven's *Eroica*:

The dream is heroic. Its drenchings in
The ears, against the cemetery's
Equivocation, we maintain it.

There is a green against blue,
Measure landscapes how you will.
A wrinkle round the neck is age.

Guess is certainty when it's love.
The gardener will vouch; two lovers
After love; the look of the lake

After wind ruffles calm slightly
And all falls into place, the blue,
The sail, the unexpected, the hills.

We come to know. Not all comes
At once. Suffering is first,
Joy and the loss of it, fact

And reduction, malice. Wisdom is
Accumulation; music is got to,
Not taken for, as everything.

Not everything falls as leaf into petal,
Apple's crimson, determination,
A door closed. Deadly cold

Is the dead touched but grief other.
Kind to kind, shark, elephant,
The heavy snail, the blonde north,

Congruence is born into; but being
Is from choice, conclusions learned.
A thousand launchings, lines, heroics,

Are Helen brought to conclusion, Kandinsky
Abstract, the moon finally Mercator's
Though silver wrinkles the lake. Fingers

Have a memory through playing keyboards.
Watch the cheesemonger judging cheese
The pound exact cut into, tobacconist

The shag, surgeon the trouble. Wisdom's
A shaping though prayers don't think so.
Failure a grandeur next time round.

Brancusi and his bird in space.
How the oriole hangs his hanging
Nest was done a million years.

Instinct is plankton, whale's mouth;
Hitler or grandeur, our own will
Shapes action. Love doing it

Is Banting and his happy isles,
Simpson with his chloroform,
The suffering knowing what hurt is;

Knowing what to die for,
The stuffed bear on the nursery floor,
The light put on to take a look—

Or Laurin strangling Mother Goose,
A spread of cant to slop the hate.
Instinct's double, pithecanthropus,

The pope shot down, through ocean
The shark's continuous movement. Love
Lacking: indifference, the deadly harm.

Ceremonies shape instinct,
Manners that are moral, the word
In action, music which is itself.

Beauty is that which is least waste,
Voltaire's garden, the sun's extravagance
Dug for, Adam when

He went to work. Commercialize
The product how we will, Noah
Builds his ark, steering the clumsy

Hulk through moral rains to heaven,
The final stranding, everything gambled
But no one in the tub wanting

The muddy inch of Ararat.
Shem trained his manners, Ham,
And Begat, and Michelangelo.

15   *Dignities are the best gamble.*

What we do is the bed we lie in.
Free will trains the id and *God
Knows* trains the will. What

Turned Ageladas to carving marble
Is anybody's guess, though
A good one is the predilections

For heaving stones at dinosaurs,
Flaking flints and pleasing surfaces
On to other famous choices

Exalting dignity until the whole thing
In a burst of genes previsions
Buonarroti. God along

The line just may have had a hand in it.
You never can tell. Hard to think
Of Jesus as out of a barn, Possums

In banks. What made Hofmann play,
Aged 4? Instinct, art,
God, morals, what priority?

16   *We have to be careful.*

But this alone be sure of: lacking
Art, a mess. Art's humanity,
And that, the way to beckoning heaven.

Torquemada the highroad? You crazy?
Wycliffe's corpse dug up and burned,
Odorous racks and Knox (delight

Slipped in in the doing) loveliness
Damned, fulmination against
A rosy complexion, the devil investing

Darwin's evolutionary fin?
What do you want? 10,000 dead,
A boundary moved a mile—Bonaparte

Out for a breather, Hamilcar's head
Heaved through a tent-flap wagging its windpipe?
Art is compassion. Lip service—

And the ills of the world are got. Piety
Is thought to be clean until you smell
The stake; theology until God's a glut.

17   *The creative act is the right one.*

Renoir sat painting, arthritic,
The brush tied to his wrist, Hopkins
Got his news of God sparring

At Manresa, Einstein made it—
Up to the count of ten over
Hiroshima when the perfumes of Arabia

Were washed away. Not God's
Doing nor truth's either, Pilate
Drying his hands while Jesus hung.

Still is Owen greater than Flander's
Mud, Chartres more than La Bourse.
Homer blind as a bat hangs

Around, seven cities claimant;
Hung up, the wrong cosmography,
Miles offcentre, Milton has earth

Dependent on his golden chain.
Mark and Luke, done in, thought it
Worthwhile. So do we.

18   *Don't believe otherwise.*

Ixion pushes his wheel, Sisyphus
His stone. We offend the gods.
Silly rows of crosses mark

The Somme. The sum of it? Not by a long shot
Though we pistol-whip old age,
Assault kids, sick minds

Ever with us. Angels still
Walk round handsomely nude on crutches.
Parked on the Parthenon, chewed gum,

One pony left on St. Mark's,
Lincoln in the White House,
Assassination on the stage,

Yet the wonder stands, Greenpeace
On the side of whales, traffic
Stopped to let the goslings cross.

X writes poems. Salk comes up
With straightened limbs and peanuts grow
In Georgia. By a long shot.

19   *The sun comes out.*

The rain came down in buckets and pails.
First the sky slate in the west,
Three splotches on the slate in the garden

Then the downpour. Green glistened,
The delphinium went to ground, the ground
Ran pure dirt, the air streaked.

Ten minutes' worth of pluvian Zeus.
Then, stop. Green glistens, leaves
Levitate, water gurgles.

Either Intelligence thought it out
Or growth adjusted, life an accident
To fact. More fun to think Intelligence

Stroked his scheming beard, belly
Generous and a cause to boot.
Lizards sliding stomachs off

An archipelago, successive Mutt
And Marx and Freud, the rabbit's ear
Evolved to the nick in the rim of our own,

Appendix by-passed as no use:
Dull, is it? Or a grandeur?
Hard to choose except that breath

Wants more than three score years and ten,
Fading snapshots in faded hats,
Jack's house, Hamlet, kids—

Never enough, what's left behind.
We need transcendence, personality
Too good to lose, bequests and wills

Trash in the purse compared to somewhere
Else, up in heaven or something
Less geographically silly.

So we choose religion, meaning
The good we do is later fun,
Pitchforks, Brueghel, notwithstanding.

To each his love.

Each here with his heaven-haven
Different. Krispies at eight, porridge
Out except for English nags,

Chopin nothing next to Vivaldi
As holes to doughnuts and solace got
Singing hymns to the cottage organ.

Gaughin said, "You paint too fast."
"You look too quick," Van Gogh. How
Reconcile Brazil with England's

Coffee? Jack loves Jill, that's
How. No accountant needed.
Cultivate the nearest garden.

22   *Low down song.*

Get out from under, that's the pitch,
Of others' bouillon keep your fingers
Out, in time get off the pot,

Thou shalt not hog the pen nor rule
The roost, let all hens cluck—once
The roosters have tread the lot. Amen.

The spray of branches coloured all
The air. May and June, apple
And twig-honeysuckle succeeded;

The male and resin-smelling spruce
In snowy woods got over winter.
Whatever greatness, up for choosing,

Choose, grandeur is not a privilege:
Crimson on the western hills
Or dawn with the west straight blue:

Paths not to be kept to, a walk
Above the lake, governance; or,
Near the margin, at night the water

An acquest of stars, no moon till later,
The silver drawn from Black Point
Down to the edge where we stood,

Shaken by a little wind,
Enough to disturb the silence, the wave
Lapping a little, the stones washed.

As you will.

In the pants pocket of god all
Things belong to each other.
What's left over is Beelzebub's.

Choose the stone-lapped lake
Full of later moon, the west
Front of Chartres thirst of mind

Can't get enough of, it doesn't
Matter, a violin's shape; the emotion
Gets to the same or nearly the same

Exaltation, depending who
You are, Pericles or a humming
Tone-deaf mason of mediaeval

Norwich. The choice is to love beauty
Or being too mealy-minded being
Unable to want it, ready to waste it.

OK. Your loss.
Have it, choose the Beaubourg's outside
Plumbing, Gibran too saccharine

To bother with Haydn. An arrangement of orts
Was Cézanne's choice—an orange orange.
Da Vinci picked God's pocket.

The function of art is to represent
God—Malraux. Carman had Him
In a trillium, Moses before

Breakfast in tablets, Mike in a slave
Of marble a doodle on its back
(Look up the doodle in Florence);

Liszt found Him in a *Totentanz*
And Shelley, not much for church,
Wordstruck changed His name, White

Radiance, he called Him. "Light tensile,
Light immaculata," snarls
Pound. While commerce jingled in

The greasy till, Billyum took up
Fishy flies casting his luck
In Ireland. Write your own ticket—

Lesbos to portly Hartford. Art
Gets the drop on Sunday or thinks
It does. The smile's on tombs at Veii.

Art is man's revenge on a hostile
Universe—Malraux again.
Stars hostile? Tear down the night,

Whip up mine? Atropos cuts
The thread, what have we got? Zero.
Heaven's draughty, the stars a mess?

So is man. This whole palaver
Is silly: He gives me boils, I'll prick
His balloon. Malraux is ineffably silly,

The universe out to get us. Jesus.
What other premise but a logic
Of stars, Palomar and praise?

"I have eaten the flame," a sacrament
Of praise, love in its guises whether
The grove is here or an emblem phallus

A circle of sun on it scratched on a rock
In Camonica; listen: snow and meltings,
Spring in runnels, the smell of the air,

Moon or lilacs, the goddess there
Or not, the ecstasy too swift to inquire.
The ocean pounds on the shale, draws,

The cave sucked with turquoise; the rock
Stands incised in the valley, the altar
Abandoned with the change of gods.

In many styles.

I have watched him putting stamps
In order, neatness of completion, his longing,
The *Bluenose* of Canada. Or take God,

His cross-examination in the dock
Acquitting Him of criminal charges; Schonberg
All the way to Iceland to see

A chessman moved—or Scott to the Pole—
Jewels and De Pachmann dining at Luchow's
Before a concert, cut ruby,

Emerald, diamonds, set out on the cloth,
The shifting colours: Chopin. The child
All day with a new stone.

Style is action shaped, structure
Done, the form without waste,
And time ordered, to rightness come.

29   *All at first was not much.*

Form out of the muddy centre.
This robins sings every evening
Over and over, he should get bored,

Liquid mellifluousness if
Not melody, a fin in muck,
Mute, before it was a bird.

Adam hadn't got to the apple
Or Newton conked on the head under
His tree by the pippin which pulled the cosmos

Together, stars, Eve, black
Holes grinding yet hopeless, suns,
Moons—Adam hadn't got

His rib out or Garbo blinked her lids,
Before God said so, Yeats, Homer,
Were primordial mud, boneshop, slurp.

30   *The Word got busy.*

Ooze on the ocean floor is history;
A prism is the shifting universe
To starstruck Hubble—numbers, immortal—

Bach rehearsing contrapuntals
On a spinster in the attic
As the housemaid told the caller.

Is Liszt holed up at Tivoli—
His princess smoking black cigars
In Rome working out theology.

Sunshaft struck through salted green,
Compounds hitched like a hooky alphabet:
Poor Tom was in pouring rain.

31   *Watch out, though. Talk is cheap.*

Words can trivialize. Be careful.
Shakespeare. High endeavour. The cosmos!
Imprecision drags a wake

Slippery as hearses, alphabet soup
Slurped in limbo. Drowsy numbness—
And the nightingale's consumptive.

O lousy aim! Ambiguous shaft!
The syllable struck by a trivial quiver!
The Word made guilty of palimpsest!

32   *Take a deep breath, this is intermission.*

...All this behind us, *revenons*
A nos meditatios, in a minute.
Apostrophes meanwhile suppressed like a ripe accordion...

INTERMISSION

164

Remark the wind. Winter was carved
In line and cornice, overhang,
As if Gislebertus were at it

Adorning Autun: devils gnawing
Jonah, a great sunflower
Overhead; the little finger

Of the angel touching Melchior
Awake, his arm outside the blanket—
Or is that Gaspar? Balthazar snores—

Sculpture on a capital—the three
Wise men, told of a star—
Their heads now kept in an ignorant casket

At bombed Cologne, frankincense
And myrrh redundant. Here
Most of the winter nothing bloomed,

The birds pecked sunflower seeds
All of Lent. An armless Nova
Scotian painted with his mouth.

34   *Anyway make love.*

Abstractions are an airy nothing.
Better to hammer studs and nails,
Sit tight and enjoy the prose

In James' prayer book. Thin sustenance,
Cartesian enthymeme for supper—
Christ took bread, Columbus an egg,

Simeon sat on a pole for years,
Miles around folk held their nose
Gazing upward at abstract heaven.

Unheard music isn't sweeter.
Not *cognito*; *amo ergo sum*,
Anonymous in his bed again.

35   *Pursue particularities.*

The rattle of trains bringing goods
From Newport, cartons of plates, unsettled
Crates of iron spare parts,

Milkcans, crossing over the crossing
In the village, two kids each side of
The running red of the freight cars,

Snoozing Cacoque up there in the caboose,
The lake blue and the orange sail
And the landscape green, a cool breeze

Out of the hot summer, as if dreaming
Of Catullus at Sirmio and that old
Hand at New Place, Stratford!

No telling. Columbus packed
His duds, importuned kings and left
For China; Thorfinn Karlsefne fell

In love with icebergs, stowed his mitts,
Mushed to Markland; Barere expires
On a piano stool playing Grieg;

The devil of course never gives up;
Byron moves his menagerie to Greece;
Beethoven across the street. Restless

Citizens, every one of them. Confusion:
Arabia hath yet its glamour and its oil,
As Tennyson quoth to Vicky Imp.

The long day wanes: the slow moon climbs,
What boots the barefoot future? Sock
And buskin on, destiny stalks

The pomp and vulgar circumstance,
Chillon's Bonnivard lightless in
His cell, Dreyfus walking circles.

Squelch. Squench. Betty rinsing
Her bras in the bathroom sink, *gemütlich*
Brahms in the groove on the stereo,

Geistliches Wiegenlied,
Rocked to slumber Mary's Son,
Bless the tree that I lie on.

Squish. Squash. Betty sweet,
Brahms' revolving *Wiegenlied,*
Undies in the pretty sink.

Heroics all over the place.

Multum in parvo. And "an ant's forefoot
Shall save you." Age managing to cross
A flat floor, Colleoni

Sitting his horse bigdeal in Venice.
Dying fingers pluck at a blanket:
I remember my mother in winter, the frozen

Sheets brought in at night bent
In the basket, the moon so cold the door-latch
Scorched her fingers going in.

Comedy—that's the thing.

Saturday was the day of celebration,
The Golden Age, Saturn's, Lord
Of Liberation. Lovers came;

Thoroughbreds mounted; spuds sprouted;
Autocracy crumbled; sails went up
The river, majestic; pinwheels spouted.

Three achieved their poem, the others
Shouted. Everything came off.
Our Lady (a little tipsy) wondered

What it was really like. Mirth
Compounded. Scheherazade gargled,
Jongleurs juggled. (No joke).

Hard to deal with, humour. Morals
Out, deliverance in. Spite
In disguise, often. The means to be mean.

Not invidious, still hard
To handle: hyenas laugh, Cheshire's
Cat, professors. Nothing so grand,

Nothing so flat. Ginsberg revises.
Gabriel blows, eternity comes...
And the sheriff beats at the Boar's Head door,

Some things are sacred. Falstaff left
At the Abbey porch. All's in the tempo.
Beethoven in braces clanging his stein

To *The Ode to Joy*, beer in the Ninth.
King Charles apologetic
To be so long a time a-dying.

To see ourselves! Lear's fool:
Misfortune funny at another door,
He takes the knocks for all of us.

41   *Grit gets in the bearings.*

Be what you wish to seem, says abstract
Plato. But a disposition of goods
Gets in these grandeurs. What breaks you up

Depends on where you sit. Chaplin
In the ring, hugging the mug
For survival, dancing the referee

In between. Never stay down
For the count of ten, said the little girl
Running nowhere, on fire with napalm,

And that Jewish kid in Warsaw
With his hands up getting
The handout. Ha, ha.

42   *Copulation is bearable.*

No wonder sex flourishes while
The world clogs and crops grow thin,
Comedy and cents combined

Can't kill it, revenue itself
Each balmy April goes to bed,
Irony non-deductible. It predates

Motherhood. Indulged, it only
Causes friction, no position
More absurd, still the only

Democratic undertaking.
Rarely love, always at
The crisis shaken by creation.

The quiet primeval tidal pool
Late in the afternoon, the sea
Withdrawn. The hot sun down, gases

And minerals collide with love. Absurd
Procedure: crampon, pick and axe,
Roped in, man on Everest!

Darwin strokes his lengthening beard;
Sistine Adam, groggy, waiting
The finger of God, usurping genes

The initiator; Romeo
A double helix—drawbridge, keep
And fortress: encapsulating protein!

A story for Munchausen: instruction
Built into wriggling sperm.
Hilarious heaven and *homo servilis*

Locked into mud, free will
An illusion...Not entirely. "Heredity
Be damned," one morning when the stars

Were dim, Augustine said. "Nuts!"
Replied McAuliffe, spending Christmas
At Bastogne in 'forty-four.

Green fronds on the bottom of the lake
Suavely swayed, stuck stones
Plunged in mud sat, the mossy

Underwater world muted
Moved-through, man, his breath held,
Hairy sex small, shoulder

And side smooth push through green
As if Eden were watery, Ararat
Intolerable, as if the first instinct

Could be regained. He turns, not
Knowing, searching where beginnings were lost,
As if that could be found.

Men have their seamark
But lungs resist, keep restless
Upward wanting, ascensions of air;

Retrievals of grace ask music,
Love vertical; on hazardous skin
Relying, ask, unnatural here,

Out of it, the crash of the sea, the meadow
Below the glacier a myriad colour,
Muddiest man importunes a grace.

46   *Flowers grow.*

A bowl of pansies holds probability.
Pansies! a sad word, wrong,
The music wrong: *pensées*,

And yet nothing of more laical majesty
Among flowers, more resolution
Of complexities, devolvements of colour,

On petal, brown cast part way
On yellow threaded darker brown;
Unalterable purple and white

Translucent almost; the green of the stem
Providing conveyances of colours
Patterned even in purpose; radiance;

Its self, not against
Its own nature brought, each
Each, the beginning taught in nothing,

Without probability the end.
Not this only, this bowl,
All things natural and for an hour belief.

173

The act only will do. A need
Of poems, a contemplation of flowers
Is a desire for the act,

Not their satisfaction, their business
In a sacrament of praise.
A fresh day can so bring longings

Only virtues will do, absorptions
Of colour, consanguinities of great
Green, identities of gold ongoings

Such as make men fools
For sun, standings on moon, on snow-
ridges breath impossible, coitions,

What sudden deliverances stand for, what
Will do so we exhaust infinite
Possibilities on acts of becoming.

This evolution a religion so that
We become one with God, what's
Out of this world a possibility

Only those not in pain
Discard easily, the consummation
A deathyard dispersal that wouldn't have built

Athens Zeus not god, England's
Cathedrals He lately dead
Not Jesus. Allah believed in,

Mohammed's footprint is left in rock.
The temple is holy to our becoming,
Each past suffering saved, the casting

Off of this unknowing to be died
For, so we become that radiance.
Joan burned. Ailerons, pansies,

Love, Francis with holes in his palms,
The Sistine roof, no answer, not certainty
Certainly, the majesty the becoming.

Mind-boggling was the day.
There was sun and a clear air.
There was no fear of heart

Or lung or joint, the beginning of the end
Anonymous, across the world no one
Was inflicting death but in three places,

The television was turned off,
The colour was highly placed, blue
With white clouds, a quick bird

Across, ruby-throated, Lear
Was read, most of the world revisited,
Delphi to go back to, Ravenna, mostly

It was the radiance of roots working, natural
Visitation, the iridescence,
Green, of a red-headed fly,

Absurdity, evolutions of
The inexplicable, tendrils, the wasp,
Unswallowable sea-urchins, and of course

The mean mean enough to sit there
Insensitive. Someone pushed a lawn-mower.
Rabelais and Jesus had just met.

Arachne challenged Athena to a weaving.
She got changed into a spider. The web
Fragile in the morning. What worth

Presumption? Actaeon staggered seen
By a prude in a pool, Midas defying
Apollo, stuck with ass's ears,

A Phrygian cap to hide the blemish,
How fool the barber? Presumptuous
Humpty sits on His wall, stubborn

Becket dead for a second Hankering.
Hurroos and -ahs you'd think by now
Would be got over, locksmiths at it,

Lathes scraping, Adam, chewing,
His jawbones full of apple in Eden,
"If we weren't so dumb we wouldn't be here."

The instant when nothing need be explained,
Without need of challenge, the existence,
When the poem is; Vlaminck,

Kandinsky withholding the stroke, the action
Of the stroke conceived; completion, the moment
Of arrival, the *Eroica* concluded, nothing

Desired nor renounced, the wanting of evil
Got through, suffering solved,
The bridge balanced, the structure, the inherence

That was in the raw stone; Alps
A map, the quarry Parthenon,
The resting-point, Joyce his *yes.*

The achieving is all.

First is the truth and terribleness
Of that Everest its beginnings beneath
The sea climbed dangerously past,

Mute forms in the night of ocean.
Then blessèd is the day,
The ordinariness of air, at morning

In the pan flopped eggs, the day
Again cloudy, clouded over,
But the rain good for the coming seedings,

The sewn grass on the terrace wall;
Better than perfection, the perfecting,
Knowing the knowing is surpassable,

Imperfection to be the awareness
If the stone is to be carved, the possession
To be had, of the entrance, of the altar.

53 *The world liberal.*

Therefore each one in his god's
Name, his paradise his own,
His imperfections a vine and a trellis,

Micah sitting with his Bible
Reading Micah, swords beaten
Into ploughshares, spears

Into pruning hooks while the kettle
Boils over and the sun comes out
And all sorts of alleviation

Batter the sense and nothing will do
But the one god picking his peas
In the garden and treading the high places,

The mountains molten for very love,
His prophet picking pods over
In a pottle, hurting no one.

54   *The graces are many and actual.*

Thus neither Nazareth nor Mecca
Nor Nara but the stag seen,
The hand-lathe across the smelling

Wood, Aphrodite's foam-touched
Toes, Uranus' spill—the grace
Actual, the cornloaves of Scotland eaten

And thirteen at supper, Judas
Necessary if there is to be
Redemption, the flaked goldleaf

Patted on Buddha, bad fortunes
Like a snow tied to his bush—
Whatever myth needed, the mind

In love, the heart its challenges met
In a candle's solace, the forehead to Mecca,
The waters gone down into.

The hand to its own work, word,
Each mind its own rapture,
The prayer chosen, the altar good.

The live moment come, as of
Full completion, evanescent,
Lasting, come from those moments

When the mind lifts compelled
By the breaking of gold, the moon covered
Then free, the heart instructed or itself

Before the lighted candle, the ikon,
The glass at Chartres; as of a great
Craft, the marble, the harmony, the line,

Only as one waits, prepared,
A lifetime of preparation,
Vacillation, intensity, achieved

As the logic achieves emotion, the stone
The slant of the cutter, the word
He who uses it; as the entry,

The love made and become the future,
Not daring but having, having prepared,
The moment enough, the god achieved.

56   *For example.*

The walk remembered—Santillana
Del Mar, shirts on the iron balconies,
Laundry, the narrow streets leading

To the open fields, the fall to the valley
Then up between green hedges; clouds,
The blue open where you pointed,

A mile to the eucalyptus grove,
To the caves, of Altamira, not knowing
What would be, colour before

The words to express it, the ceiling ochre,
Red, umber, drawings on the rock,
Miracles not seen in the cave's dark.

57   *Haphazards or planning.*

The accidental; over snow
The petal in the crevice, pink filaments
On white, the flower where it shouldn't be,

Answering sun. Why, then,
The universe no less responsive,
Configurations of stars, of the world:

A spool of green thread at the side of
Uncut grey cloth;
Histories on a strange street,

Boulevards, breath held.
Recognitions not set,
Gone to, at the side of the Abbey,

Caxton and his alphabets.
Haphazards, transmutations, at the bottom
Of the rounded glass, gold.

Design all over the place.

A rufous-browed hemispingus
Came to my garden. Ornithologists
With spy-glasses it sang to.

Across the white expanse of the page
An i crawled, where it stopped,
As if copulating, it bends, digs.

Aeons God contemplated the design.
Torquemada tore it to precepts.
Virtue in the aggregate shortened it.

The universe is up to something.

The diverse workings of natural selection
That supply men with metaphysics,
Aristotle his goggles, black

Holes for Copernicus, are up to something.
Down the speedway at Cincinnati
Cars chew fronds and fossils

Unstepped on on K2.
All's one: Nureyev and his dance;
The clown-fish wiggle in coral. Not

To forget corporate man of course,
Big-wheel at the whistle-stop,
Fat chance at the crossroads.

Consider the diameter of the circle divided
Into the circumference: decimal points
Hellbent forever that the poem

Consists of, MacNeice walking down
The streets of London with stub and scribbler,
Linnaeus examining God's flies.

That the statement have reference to experience,
That the vision has been earned, that irony
Validates the metaphysics—

Einstein playing his Stradivarius
At Alamogordo the almighty speed
Of sunshine overtaking man;

The bishop shocked when Dr. Johnson
Kicked the churchyard stone—we are brought up
Short. That abrasion refine philosophy

Jills and Hijacks spray the lead:
P.p.p.p.p.p.
"Motherhood" called on, children starve

And rhetoric turns the other cheek
Though Ford and Brezhnev at Helsinki talk
In dulcet tones of kingdom come.

And they jumped in the water, the kids, splashing
Around the edge of the Nile, sunset
At Aswan over the cavern tombs and

Elephantine, burning crimson above
The island mausoleum, within,
The Aga Khan so fat he couldn't

Do up his shoes now not worth
A diamond. Reflections streak across
From the western shore to the yelling kids,

The pleasure-floating *Isis* docked
On the evening Nile, Hilton's barge,
The oil-slick waters off the stern

Melting with colours beggaring description,
On the bank the old man fishing in papyrus
Reeds, dreaming Egypt's dream,

Lotus white for the temple pools
Of Hathor cow-eared goddess of love,
The waters, shaken, riddling his pole,

Coins from the deck dived under to,
Silver slowing, snails bearing
Schistosomiasis mating, the great dam

Flooding the sedges of gold, Abu
Simbel raised to the shaft of the sun,
At midday locked in the riddling dark.

No less than joy, the casual year
Holds unnoticed autumn's end,
The sun's unconfidential meaning.

Devices of morning share a devious
Green, wind turns the silver
Questioning of leaves; the air, provisions

Of a farther sound. Histories
Come to mind, how expectation
Proved a postponed season, spring's

Delinquency a theft and breaking
Ocean not another shore,
The brilliant ground, an end to day.

Tracings of the wave withdrawn
Remain, an edge of gold; plundering
Sands abuse the line of foam;

Silence holds, the poise nearing,
Then, balance come, the fall,
Sand slapped packed to the scuff

And sedge. The spiral of a shell held
Listened to, Aphrodite
And memories of the sea a possible

Music, nothing. Off Fiji,
Yasawa, palms slanting with shadow
The beach walked on, at the ocean's

Edge a drift of sea shells,
Coral, fluted, fan, nacre
Cool to the unforgetting hand,

Of no memory except the thumb
Smooth with them, only the wave breaking,
The rock cave holding dark

Where now the entering fullings wash—
Yet ocean meanwhile, sun, wave,
On the sand, washed tides, shell.

And so the moment is all, neither
Desire nor repugnance except for the want
Of waste, the hurt assigned, another

His love denied, his difference decried;
Peace in the avenue of elms, autumn's
Turning, the ridge of the valley come

To the westering sun, the interim our
Design, insistence of our dream
To tell what was, what is to come,

Finally that which we do. Only
The praise of love, the humour gained,
The permanence of temporary gods.

1984
DIRECTIVES OF AUTUMN

Eyes and ears are bad witnesses
if the soul is without understanding.
—HERACLITUS

Wheel of Fire

The endless search, question—all
The transgressions: beyond the farthest sun
Hubble guessing another galaxy,
And as at Ayers Rock that time
The star that fell almost at your feet,
And happiness at last transferred to a silicon
Chip—the axis ever turning,
Place without station except
It's in heaven and that no satisfaction,
No astringent and sweet earth
To get down to—this is what is
Whether mind itself disprove it:
Heavenborn *jubilate!*
Until the gate slams, turned
Against the hinges' rid grate.

Man Untestamented

Think of the orchid and the white fantail
That toppled the world. It was, after all,
Not Lucy the hominid but the boggy
Sundew, the short legg'd pigeon
And frivolous finch that led Darwin to truth
More upsetting than he had bargained for.
Alas for the instant literalist.
He was born not in the image of God,
He developed fins and perched trees.

                                   What
A way to proceed! By daft detail not
Testaments. Unregenerate man,
A consort of pigeons, a graduate of gills,
Rank pick-up of passion and dirt.

The Nature of Existence

The point-blank and ultimate friction
Should sustain us but it fails,
Being, in bed, the window-blind
Snaps up and there is dawn—

The ability to view the bed.
Thought's a cathedral making greenest
Moss confess and breaking combers,
A gasp to the exultant flesh,

Considerations of wind and weight.
The mind is a reading about it:
Cleopatra passing intangible
Pearls in soluble goblets

Around the banquet hall. Books.
Eating popcorn at *La Bohème*
The orchestra soaking the abstract ears,
Body and soul both, is the only

Rig and brave to go in:
The way the darling nun marries
God as God looked down and took
The handful nearest Him of dust.

Statement

The bee examines the frame glasses
Placed on the slate coping of the garden
Retaining wall looking for honey.
The appeal isn't right, the smell
Wrong. The scarlet of the flower petal
Nearby seduced him but the spectacles
Sidetracked his sensors, something
New. Less pollen will be spread—
As if an abstinence for the night.
Not that either much matters.

The bee moves off and a translucent
Hummingbird moves into the scene,
A whirring like a deathly standstill.
He drinks, agglutinating pollen.
Another bee or perhaps the same one
Goes off, sides sticky.

Abundance is at work, frustration
Is at work. It all works out. He
Loves his wife up to the deadline,
The bee goes to his hive honeyed.
Next year is accomplished.
There will be much to learn about.

Impromptu

On winter's afternoons I light the wood cuts
When the sun goes down. My thoughts are heavy.
Memento homo—remember, man, thou art
Mortal, even now the water's lake
Is frozen over, even now no faith
Will save the sun from going down. *Morte!*
As they say in Verdi's operas, the hero
Crossing swords with baritones in likely
Graveyards, praying heroines on their knees
In chastity. Oh well, the fire burns.
I set the match to Montreal's *Gazette*
Laid over by the kindling birch and flames
Arise. I heat my buttocks backside to
The fire a hitch to warm the chilly light
Then turn away, reality in my ears.

This has modulated to lethal metre...

How else should the piece conclude?
I am open to suggestion, meanwhile
Hug my gloom and think of miraculous fishes.
This life is full of short oblivions.

The Mind Needs What the Poem Does

White lilacs and Berlioz—
Take them as standing for the world and what
We make of it. Say it is Berlioz' opera
Les Troyens, and let us say
They are white lilacs clipped from the bush
That last afternoon of May;
With late evening, the dark fragrance
In the room and burning Troy.
Which was as real as the other?
What man creates in meaning is
The world we live in though the rocky
Earth is what we ride on. Flowers
At the cost of wooden horses: heroic
Foolishness.
               Stars we got free.
Fashioned, finagled implements—
A door-hinge, wheel, straight nails—
Worthier than the starry night,
What we make of them are histories.

More than themselves, lilacs are amorous
Troy; lacking the town, abstract
Music is a competent mockery.

"Café du Soir"

All this uproar under the stars
Only art makes sense of. The houses
Pay no heed to the passing night,
The moon is an object—it takes art
To get to the bottom of it. Men
Hate one another. The uproar
Of consent tingles the pulse. This
Disbelieved, ask the next
Person. The noise assails the ears.

Let us refer to those two at the café
Sitting outside in the night, the electric
Bulb bare, the street past the chairs
Empty, they tolerate one another
Only because of Van Gogh's paint.

Variations and Fugue on a Theme of Handel

Brahms turning Handel
Into Brahms. That's newness!
Surely as that bough
Shaken of petals comes
To summer, those turns baroque
Lift into largeness, spacial
Variation. Two
Against three the rhythm (*there!*)
Nothing to do with Handel;
Harmony not thought of, yet,
As a theft of poetry, his—
Even that silence new!

Stolen music ever
Hostage to those petals
On that bough, a shoal
That strands the heart; as
It was, newness ours.
Listen! Triumph, that change
Next to the final fugue!

In Santa Prassede, Rome

I   The Chapel of San Zenone

The lights came on, flooded the green
And scarlet edges, mosaics of flakes
Of gold, the small chapel flooded
Where journeymen from Byzantium adjusted
Arch and doorway, adorning faith
With lambs and leggy heron grazing
God's pasture, the palms of four
Archangels' feet on the curving world,
Pinched Jesus in the vault of the dome.

     O love and love! lost to the violent
Times, the reasonable world unravelled,
The sinking silly church still promising
Remission from mediaeval Hell—
Ten years remitted to each
Pilgrim here who says three *Pater
Nosters* over.

           Blind sadness!
The Roman column Jesus was lashed on
Brought from Jerusalem a harrowing here,
Herod's crucial judgment beaten.

     Only art grips the soul—
These scintillant million pieces, mosaic
Workings, silly pastures, vaults
And vaultings pasted up with love.

Never mind. We have them...

Even the bird on the palm-tree has a halo
Around him, the Saviour points to it, if
You believe in haloes and saviours. So. The world
Wags or doesn't according to what man
Does to himself or doesn't. I stand down
Here at the chancel steps in doubt of man,
His sanctimony shows, I have seen enough of him.

    I turn to the chapel of San Zenone again,
At the side—where the apple mosaics and the plants
And the deer reside in green—where Teodora,
Her halo square since that lady was yet alive,
And the twelve gentlemen demonstrate faith
And the toenails of the angels are dirty and all
Is slightly comedy and easier to take—
Faith with two grains of salt and myself
Most of all with a whole bag of it.

Ceremony Is Called For

Not only
Is it gloss for the death of the dead,
Is ceremony churchyard silence for horny feet,
The living must have it.
Lacked swaddling roses two days gone,
Laced in sea-bags minus silks,
Still is the stiff to be dumped with dignity.
How much more those
Oppressed.

Let us have ritual, manners,
Post the conclusions
And rehearse our rubrics, deodorants and god.
Ceremony ennobles all.

The Day Was One Of Sun

This glorious sun confounds the end
Of August. What a cue is this day
Despite Syria and serious sequences!
I suppose the sun shines in Lebanon
As well, on Persian lilac, the curly
Karakul. Love is possible. Lucky
With Canada, proximities of northern seas,
Prosperous summer's federation,
This day is for true devotion, adherences
Whose accurate accounting proves the worth
Of love. But whether good and good
Are in sequence—yesterday's newspapers
Lighting winter's fires, cool
Melons piled in Samarkand—
Keep in mind. You can't tell.
What we have is what we were born to.

This window looks westerly—five
Crows sit across the cropped
Field mute, waiting for white
Snow not there to apprehend...

The Broken Pianola

Walt Whitman's postmortem brain was accidentally
Dropped by an assistant on the laboratory floor...
What contusions, what measurements, what battering
The human brain is butt of! Convolutions
That roil up spring and the winter weather
Into landscapes for a million loves
That live in sticky lyrics—halves out for
Adherences, glue for the tragic pieces—little
Thinking *plop*, all that poignance: porridge
On the sterile floor! What measurement of Einstein's
Cranium-fill could halt an altercation?
They pickled his as well as Walt's. O problems
And O poems!

       Digress a moment. Think of
The first flush of that assistant: *Good god,*
I've dropped it!

       There Whitman lies.

... Something's happening to this poem.
The hurt of a victim intrudes, Argentina's
Latest, Russia's Jews, what breaks the tune?
After so many the millionth is trivial.
Anonymous, forgotten, persistent, the image—
The image of that millionth in his cell
Sitting amidst his defecations, his
Ironic comedy. What have we left to go on
But Whitman's brain on the laboratory floor?

But there He sits, Jesus amidst his body's
Spill: the latest media news preventing
Pontius going about with mop and pail...

202

Stained Glass

The halt and lame, what to think about them,
The girl
Hanging on the arm of the older woman
Walks the cathedral floor with a lilt.
The legs won't work, the muscles of the hip
Won't work properly. They tilt her.
She'll never get a love. The organ heaves.
She stares angled at the glass,
Reds, green, gold,
A rudeness. Her two braids
Swing as she goes on holding on.
She was not born right. The seeding was wrong.
The world tilts.

Bourges Cathedral

State of Affairs

This is a world of small boys with legs off.
Hip. Hip. They walk the world grown up.
Bitterness is not unknown.

Of course always there have been legs off
In a manner of speaking, taking legs off
To stand for eyes out,

But that is expected—the previous century is barbaric,
Few university degrees were granted,
TV was unknown.

It is too bad since we have so many computers,
So many carbines and combines that we have
So many legs off

But it can't be helped, boys must hop as best
They can, bitterness or not, there must be legs off
So there can be progress,

That is to say democratic election,
Culture for the collectivity and less
In the future legs off.

Mutual Assured Destruction

Hard to think of it,
What was loved, as too
Bad. Hard to think
He who cares for his neighbour's
Children, he will be
Only too happy
To get it over,
Fit the lock,
The damned
Red phone slammed
Down, done with, God
So loved the world
Had up to here.

Prose note: as MAD stands for "mutual assured destruction,"
GROB, the Soviet acronym for civil defence, is also Russian for "coffin."

Anatomy of Melancholy

It was a silver sky. Silver
Over the lake and at the edge
Of the horizon of hills. Clouds,
Sooted clouds spoiled the silver,
In streaks. No stars were about,
It was too early, dusk held
But far in the west, toward the south,
Somewhere the sun was still up. Cold
Came. It was winter, a sky
That was winter.

                    Again,
There was news. The marine
Caught in the fall of stone
Was on his back, the way
He had been placed, naked
From the waist up, his arms
Over his head, the mark
Of hair underarm black
But below, below the chin,
Pulp of red, a great contrast
Of where the world was wounded
And where it wasn't.

                    Winter
Didn't have much to do with it,
He being in the east where the sun
Is perpetual or pretty much
All the time. But the cold sky
Lent a melancholy, a melancholy
The natural feelings of well-being,
Or at least a semblance of well-being,
Could not overcome. Otherwise
Winter was alright, was natural.

The Absurdity

And time shall make it unimportant,
The tragedy, the fall from grace,
The slump in the back-seat,
The spout off the garden watering-can unexpectedly
Dowsing the *fragilia*, and the headstone at a jaunty
Angle. We are told, *Keep your thoughts on heaven,*
Grief is not there. They did, think of
The prayers that went up in the fourteenth century
What with Black Death and cathedrals. Don't
Worry too much about the cancer,
Think of the number of them you don't
Care about.

            It helps to think
This way. It eliminates everything
Eventually, what matters
Not excluded, how Christ hung,
Whether through the wrists or palms,
And what to do with the future.

Aspect of a Cut Peach

Succulent as morning were the pieces of that peach.
Cut on the china plate of mint foliage
Around the rim, a cool gathering circle
Of indentation holds the fragments of quench
And question. What has this to do with hunger
And Ethiopia? Rotten weather in Ontario
Raised the rarity of that peach. The skin peeled
Back like a nonpresbyterian pleasure,
What of the cry of children that runs off
The guilty blade of silver? Heaven is doomed
Here. Only in paradise are peaches
Prized purely and is pith succulent.

To Simon Wiesenthal

It's the dignity accuses:
The shoulder bones
In outline,
In quiet outline, the look
Reaching through the barbed wire,
The barbed wire.
Not until the G.I. walked through
Carefully not to disturb
The inmate washing his shirt
Over again in the pail
Did the world get it. Messages
Of dignity, bare
Dignity,
Are hard to get over
To people
Shouting.
Eventually it is heard.
It is heard eventually.

The files are to be found
In a three-room occupancy
In Vienna.

Don't Listen Wholeheartedly
to the Poets

It's the open-endedness ought to be eliminated.
Walt Whitman stomping around,
"Very well then I contradict myself.
I am large, I contain multitudes."
All equal is nothing of value.
Advocacy is not "a blurt."
This ought to be clear.
And cross your fingers listening to
Graveyard Eliot and better Pound,
To Holub opening his hollow door:
That it is better to do anything
Than nothing.
Goebbels nearly made it.

The Road by the Lake

Cars pass along the road.
The moon is caught in the branches of the birch
Bare of leaves, only the lower right arc
Thin as an edge, is visible, the rest
Imagined so that the weight in the branches
Is heavy and is bent gold.

Over all the scene, a quiet
Despite the road's intrusion. It is an emotion
Not unusual if a lake is there
And hills, some few to contain the sadness,
The sadness of life (for life is sadness
Whether the city or the successful hills).

Melancholy is not unavoidable
But there are certain things: the certainness
Of what is said; the commonness that changes
Name only. The mist that is come
Over the moon is an example of what
I mean—but that is not it:

The present commonness and the cost:
Great agreements spent on the trivial—
Men who speak of what is easy—
Who honour it and the force of violence—
O all who travel this lakeside road
And are under the diminished arc of this moon.

I would have common kindness and high art,
Not what all would understand
At once but could strive for, awakening
To wonder and achievement, and a certain honour
For those who only love—a quiet
Road beneath whatever moon.

Through Clear Crystal

Through clear crystal the sun's rays
Shall break, break in colours.
The force of light shall see to it.

Though the wave break on long shores
The seas shall be no less, logic shall prove it
And the weight weighed in handfuls.

Your love is constant though cold death is in it.
Nothing shall harm it, not years and oppositions,
Not seasons and their dispositions. Nothing will.

It is given and once given and made whole by gift,
Nothing shall take it away or diminish it being.
Love is an eternal so given and is death itself.

Hearing the Woodthrush
in the Evening

Through the screen-door in the early night,
The song of the thrush. After sundown
He sings. I listen and the wonder is not
Of one song, exactness is about me,
The truth of the world that even as the heart
Responds exactness comes, such as
Music loved and heard again
Provides and love provides, no sooner
We turn from the lake where the moon is
Than the glory of a night without moonlight
Is remembered glorious with fallen stars
Reflected—nothing of our own making
(As being in love, sensitive for the moment,
Or in the compensation of a remorse
Or in the tyranny of other happening)
Grace of itself, renewed,
The short phrase of the nightthrush
All over again we can hardly take it.

There! again. In the falling night—
The tragic song coming through
The kitchen-screen where I stand—
Repeated though I had not asked.

The Question of Winter

The snow is heavy on the hedge,
Everywhere is white, burdened
With beauty brief as this cloudy day,
But here, now, the long hills
Bending, the mountains, the spruce by the house,
At night a gold window in it,
The cedar and bare maple all over
With fallen glory far from April.

This asks answer, the grand gesture,
Of us, the earth rolling, blue,
Whirled cloudy blue from the viewpoint
Of the moon, this blue earth
With winter on it: What of that agreement
To miss out? What has it, that other
Season of yours when here now
Is snow along the hills, the road,
That cancellation is never made
In the insistent heart and its involvement
Held-to, though the moment is now,
In what is gone, in what will come?

Assertion About Winter

For winter isn't always strict.
Children in two sweaters and mitts
Love it,

Countrymen with sleighs of wood
Go up the hill on foot
Easing horses,

Blowings of frost at their nostrils.
There is an ease, weights of snow
Sliding off.

Wives look out of lighted windows
At evening. Chilblains are not
Unknown at rinks

But youths with girls go around
Scuffing crust on hard surfaces
And at appropriate times

Men with fishing-lines in wind-
shelters outsit temperatures,
Meanwhile

Counting stars that come on. Actually
Strictness is often economical,
Not much said,

Those with lucky burning fireplaces
Hoarding up silence. Outside, northern
Lights sometimes

Play above roofs. It has been known
That front doors possess deliberate paths
To them.

Lilies at Mount St. Helens

Avalanche lilies break the earth,
Bugs appear at St. Helens.
Life returns.

I walk this path pumice-covered,
Fern and lupine cling
The banks; above the

Persisting world snow glistens.
I pluck a blade to show
I control mortality.

Death has nothing new to show for it
But the glory of renewal,
David's descent,

This Easter. I accept the ancestry; look down:
Above, the glory of uncertainty,
At my heel, white lilies.

In the Everglades

All animals are holy,
They are themselves.

The birds are sacred,
The sky theirs.

The heron stands for hours
On one leg

And the roseate spoonbill
Seeks side to side.

The alligator eats once a week
And slides in

And among the mangrove roots
His small one waits.

A movement! The watcher
Adjusts his lens,

He does not know why
But feels worship,

That fat woman feels worship,
And the camper, and the baseball

Cap, and bright eyes.
No one speaks:

The egret is beautiful and the blue
Heron and the ibis.

No one can say why.
Each is itself.

The people do not move,
Each in identity.

At the Zoo

O for all the blind, sadness!
For all men, reminder, reminder,
Light is done, eyes do not see,
Girls walk by grace of others,
Hands reach out, rain falls
And leaves do not show silver, the eyelid
In its workings clears nothing.
Praise, those who count suns.
Children. Children. I think of children
Not used to it, a happening
Of birthdays felt only,
Neither red, nor yellow, nor white
Candles—except the heart convey it.
In this smelly yard, small
Hands discover the elephant, the entire
Enormous building, rumpled skin
Going up forever standing still,
The soft snuff dangerous but the movable
Ears flopped with withdrawals not really.
I watch the stupendous information.
Elephant is said to be there.

Timbres

I Castanets

Castanets are an instrument of the dry months
At river banks of the clack of women washing, arising.
They have gained some currency at court.
Hidalgos in high places are amused.
They chatter of broad backs and breeding.
Women washing observe the bulls above clatter,
Whacking Castile clotheswater.
It is the violin that is elegant.

II Toccata

The north makes an aesthetic difference.
Its worth is not to be diminished,
It is a corrective of artistic concerns.
Perspectives from the sheer ice the red sun
In radiance loosens
Lean seaward.

Silence rides the broken spray.

In the south
Moonlight plucks an indolent mandolin
Deckling the edge of ancient nights.
A breeding is heard in the shadows.
The stars' design heavily depends.

Of the Laurentian north the stops are of woodwind.

The music is of the exact piano.

Ogunquit Beach

I *Wind Surfacing*

The thousand people are going to die.
The sun is out,

kites are in the sky, coloured,
green with scarlet tails,

the baby in the crawl-crib
squalls at the canine,

quits, chewing the indestructible
plastic ring. Girls rub

oil on against cancer, the
life-guard watches.

All the world thrives, waves
shatter and the beach adjusts.

Danaë combs her hair;
Time is in the tower.

Everybody is going to die.
Crosslegged

beneath the umbrella the men
slap down cards,

draw, jockstrap
trumps the ace of spades.

It is impossible that blue
sail can stay upright.

II *Kites*

Three kites I thought were birds
Until riding a rite of air
One slipped and was onion and green,
The tail of an extraordinary balance.
One tugged an invisible string.
The third tried to get off the ground.

I fell in love with discovering this.
No perfect bird is worth this love
Having to make it, creating, running
Topaz and green aloft there
And the delicatest wind taken
Advantage of and carved accordingly.

III *Cliché*

The chaos of gulls
Settles on the refuse.
One with a yellow
Hooked bill
Keeps trying to
Haul out of
The blue container
The rectangular lid
Of a shoebox.

The man can't make firm
His striped umbrella
To the arm of his chair.

The child in front of
The pool that was left
Builds a barricade
Against the tide.

The new girl
Keeps combing her hair
The wind blows back.

IV *That Green Fire*

The fixed grass of the dunes
Looks like blown smoke.
That green fire is forever.

It is still then blows fiercely
Tethered as the day. The sea-crests
Break. The eternally broken fence

Tugs wire people always
Get through. The woman bather
Has difficulty with her fat ass

But makes it. The attempt is lovely.
The wind in the grass dunes is lovely.
The broken fence is lovely.

V *Sunday*

The beach is crowdeder than ever.
Humanity swamps everything,
Rocks lugged, anchor what's taken off,
Sat on. Legs are established. Cokes.

Across the dunes on the empty bay
The solitary dissident sits
In the canoe he can't manage.

VI *Night*

Three people walk watching
the waves. All day
it has rained, it stopped only
with the moon out. One
light is in the distance,
in the house three miles
down the grass dunes.
The father wears an orange
raincoat, one of the kids
doesn't care, the other
does. They walk beyond
the corner of the beach-
house, the high moon
on the ebb of the ocean, glimmers.
The day is gone. The grey
gulls have the place to themselves.

Five Transparencies

I *Tao In North Hatley*

Picking red currants by the western hedge
I catch a glimpse of the silver lake
Every once in a while as I raise my body
To ease the muscles of my thighs and back.

The unknown bird sings and then stops.
I listen to the sudden silence,
Then begin picking red berries again,
Dropping them in the deep pan with the handle

Brought from the kitchen. Fingers of both hands
Are stained with the red juice, some
Of the berries are very ripe. I like
The stain. I am one with the bird again

And the quiet reminds me of that scholar, Tao Qian,
In his garden tending his fourth-century
Chrysanthemums, eighty-eight days
Out of the court and its weary obeisances.

Among these hedges and the red currant bush
In the corner, apart, listening to the bird
And picking berries, I too have a fundamental
Truth to tell if only the words could be found.

II *Of Lu Hong the Scholar*

For his learning and integrity Lu Hong
Received from Xuan Zong his emperor
One hundred pecks of rice
And fifty bolts of silk.

His thatched hut on Mount Song
Had a brook, a bridge to cross it,
And a glass house, not large,
To care for delicate seeds.

Ten views of Lu's hut
Are still to be seen with poems to go
With each view well apart
From the purlieus of the court.

III *The Story of Wang Wei*

More elaborate was Wang Wei's eighth-century villa.
Rambling houses, pavilions and galleries
Connected by bridges and paths (famed
Among architects)

Imposed neither isolation nor abnegation.
Wang was no happier but he had
Many perspectives to describe with ink and colour
On rice paper.

He commanded visual inspiration walking
His courts and gardens. He was wise
However. Dynasties of vast wealth
And pleasure foundered

On unrestrained expenditure. (By the third century
Gardens were already synonyms for extravagance.)
Wang walked his garden paths laughing
At the intricacies.

226

IV   *The Opinion of Ji Cheng*

A better view even
Than you would have
Sitting in trees,
Says Ji Cheng the author
Of a treatise on gardens,
Is through the moon gate,
The far willow in it,
And across the lotus pond
Where the blossom
Unfolds, from the mud,
Unstained petals.
All this even in the midst
Of a marketplace!
Noise is shut out
When the gates are closed,
Notes Ji in his book *Yuan Ye*.

V   *At the Orchid Pavilion*

Amid the harshness of pebbles
My reluctant feet wander,
At sundown I sit by the willow
Listening to the plucked lute.

Debussy: Three Nocturnes

I *Nuages*

The horizontals merge and undulate.
One colour, one colour!
On the *Pont de Concorde*,
Clouds, clouds in the sky
Sweep slowly, sway,
My heart is with her.
Is with her.

II *Fêtes*

Oranges, lemons, crabs,
Mackerel with heads on,
Fresh shrimp! All along
The *rue de Seine*
Mesdames sell and yell
Good goods, *asperges*
Fresh from the country!
Noise, noise! My heart
Caught but still hers,
I turn from potatoes and spinach.

III *Sirènes*

Voices and song. O soul,
The world is a hurrah.
Yes, yes, my love beside me,
The world is a great burst
Of ahs, O a great burst of hurrahs!

For a Moment, the Act

I look up from the words and see the near heavens—
Not the celestial but clouds white and separate and cumbrous
On blue, and trees in sun, sensations of
Earth, deep green and deep blue.
Death is not written on twice.
Listen. The catbird even is mixing it up.
The big fly pulls a thread of whine across.
The sky has a hole. I breathe without causing it.
Summer is short (it is summer). Why is no good.

Crescendo

What seems the world is fallen,
the world is fallen,
leaves are caught around what is made, the chair,
leaves are caught in the branchings of grass
and the stalks of the last flowers,
the whole day goes down in foliage,
the sun across the leaves strikes gold not to be
confused with connotations, April,
only the chrysanthemums open from cold buds of bronze,
the dark casing too late for the trust of the world.
                    Each way is scuffling.

Hunter's Moon

The moon was gold and the leaves were gold.
The red leaves had fallen and the pallor
Of the soft aspen was lighted, as gold,
By the hunter's moon, the first full
Moon of October. She stood on the verandah,
Facing that upper gold moon
(My arms lightly, closely around her
As if the time would come now).
Foliage was fallen thickly, the lawn
Uncertain, the dry brown leaves
Fallen. Across the pathway
The last flowers, a further frost
Was promised.

        She did not like the deer
To be in the forested hills. It is a hunter's
Moon, she said. But it was beautiful,
The dense covered hills, the moon above,
The moment, the way it was,
The moment.

Last Poem

Snow piles, the rails
Will hardly sustain it, dusk
Falls over the country.
There will not be birdsong.
Small matters make
History—the song of a bird,
Snow again falls.

Summer will not return,
That which was known.
Though the earth turn,
That which was known and believed
Is taken and is gone.

1985
TWELVE LANDSCAPES

Twelve Landscapes

I *The Geography of Grass*

These longitudes cross
At Ellesmere's icy drift,
Scott's Antarctic walk.
They enclose the globe.

Here, the apple blooms,
My curve of line goes north
Through Baffinland. I am
High up on it.

The blossom scatters in the green
Cascade I walk through
Where I cut the grass.
I trim oblivion.

Again the tanager returns,
His brief descent of scarlet
Marking the slender chance
To his summer place.

I free the blades, the bottom
Edge caught on a knuckle
Of twig. The thrown tangle
Praises my feet.

And the Trento farmer washing his grapes,
Each side the spray washing.
Across the world the trellis holding
Flowers

Notable for honey-combs. Midnight
Floods the northern Cape with sun.
The bending wader plants his rice;
Porcelain

Temple-bells where the Chao Phya
Flows, slanting, touch. Hot,
The lonely sands at el-Amarna
Are hot.

The train draws slowly up
The Pass. At the frontier, snow
Falls. The glacier holds the last of
Sun.

Three hours it took to save
The world, no more; a woman
Dying happy, two men
Fishing.

III *Still the World, at Dusk*

I push aside the curtain of the window
To see the glory of the world—
Not so far aside that the bare
Street bulb on the corner telephone
Pole spoils the dusk. I have watched
Beauty. The Massawippi hills
Are black against an orange sky
Going amber—the darkening north
Blue, one piercing star, mighty
Jupiter, in it northwest
Of the lower moon. The world is glory—
Without man remembered in it—
I mean, man not remembered except
His irony gone brave: Chaplin's; Falstaff
Outrageous in Eastcheap, trying on
Crowns on kitchen chairs, he
And old Shallow hearing chimes a-midnight.
Otherwise loving Falwell or Khomeini
Loathing to have the riffraff in Teheran
Touch him, is what you get.

                              It's dark.
The colour has gone, Jupiter still
Up, silver still—but not
Much else of note, worthy of words.
Night comes: the Bologna train
From Florence about to be blown up
Enters the tunnel; Falwell proclaims
Exclusive ownership of God.

IV *Hundreds of Crocuses*

A defiant spread of crocuses, jagged,
Noble, everywhere in interstices
Of soil between rocks, showed,
Indifferent—oh indifferent. Whether
Prophecy had god, had doom in it
To come, they exulted, white,
Purple, stamens gold, six petals,
Unknown except you bend down to it,
But colour far, near, some yellow,
Out of the debris of April roots
And marks and tendrils left the snow gone.
Nobility was there to see, never
Mind resurrection, beauty
Was here.

       A patch of landscape,
An acre.
    I gazed.

You looked again and to the right, behind,
A bunch of crocuses grew there.

v *The Wheatfield*

To stand alone in a field of wheat.
Sun brushes husks, the movement
Of the field hovers in the wind.

Alone, for this is the condition: to know
The maturity of all things
And have no answer, no command

Of love declaring permanence,
Of being without separation,
The alliance solace to an irony,

Alone with the lost experience only.
Break off the thinking... The sun is hot,
The wheatfield smells of coming harvest.

Look, you have had love and though
Now alone, the birds are swift
In the grain where the ripe fulness is,

Without that memory you would not have had
Being, being here without
Submission would be a bitterness.

VI *At the Oceanside*

It is too bad, the unending sloven.
Look, this little girl and boy,
Nothing on, strut utterly
In beauty, pails in their hands hauled
Splashing to castles. The beach is crowded
With citizens, once (misfortune apart)
With loveliness, now not once
Regretting nothing of it, their grandeur,
What they have made of it.

The truth denied.

Where the kiteman sells his kites,
A coloured one with tails is held
At the tip by the tiny one, blonde as the wind
And sand, two feet high, till the tremble
Takes it up to the sky and clouds.

VII *One Cannot Overcome the Nature of Happiness*

Chestnuts roasted, snow falling,
To this day are loneliness.
No matter the crowd at 55th and
Sixth, the busy tapping their heels
At noon on the balustrade of the fountain,
The wind cold from the west, from the Hudson,
The charcoal brazier making bravely
Warm the southwest corner of the street,
No matter possessing love, chestnuts
In a paper bag, hard coals,
Pink steam at the corner of the city,
      a loneliness inextricable
Is in the awareness of heart that all
This world is gone. Is it not so—
That what you love is its moment gone?
How could it be otherwise, this possible
Glory: November, the pavement, Luigi
Old, his chestnuts eight for a dollar,
The snow falling, the street forever—
No escaping that wind, from the Hudson?

VIII *The Ribbon*

And there, was a November moon, enormous,
Exactly round, flat, pasted
On the evening sky, low down,
Held immense before me east
Along the road between two banks
Of piled snow to the turned end,
The near lake steaming in zero;
South were hills, the valley changing,
One long streak of grey through the red,
One star, above, increasing;
Oh a thousand aggregations
Made impact on me as I walked
But one notice only, halfway
Up the hill, remains as it was:
Where two fir trees are,
Tied to a strand of wire, on the fence,
Marking importance, ribbon, forgotten.

IX *Counterpoint*

The mushrooms simmer in the pan.
The mountain is there
eternal in snows.

There is magnificence everywhere.
The climber slowly climbs,
cleats hold, the grandeur does not come down.

The aroma of mushroom excels the taste.

What care was taken!
The blood in the veins is returned to the heart.
The roped mountaineer crosses the bergschrund,
the sixth camp placed, the wind gauged.

    The moon over the mountain.

    There it stands, the mountain.

The moon slowly crosses the kitchen window.

x *Mid-Winter, Indoors that Night*

'And the moon went down on the temple that was.'
Michelangeli playing the piano.
Meaning, meaning is the only reality!
The music as it is! All
That evening was greatness, bells traversed
The foliage, Debussy's little girl
Sang to her sleepy doll;
And those hours when the meaning
Was an old man deaf in Vienna.
We do not listen.

                    Outside
There is the constant howl of wind,
Down the Massawippi Valley.
The soul ceases for a moment. The longing
Comes for that which is not heard...

XI *Late February*

This February afternoon is grey
And miserable and you move like a legend
Children love. I adore you.

When will it cease, this dirty snow
And rain? I remember Maui where
You watched night-blooming cereus.

Where are the days gone and what
Does it matter—the year's decline?
The fire burns well in the room,

You putting fresh sheets
On the floor from the washer to dry and moving
As though this poem was as important

And the birds at the feeder are seed-crazy.

XII *Ingonish*

And the wave breaks on the rock,
Spray to the sky, colour,
Rainbows, rainbows!
And the power and terror:
Listen!
The cliff where the curlews cry,
The spray
Smashed in glory, the rock in glory!

Index

Titles, Sub-titles or First Lines

Also by Ralph Gustafson

Poetry

The Golden Chalice   1935
Alfred the Great   1937
Epithalamium in Time of War   1941
Lyrics Unromantic   1942
Flight into Darkness   1944
Rivers among Rocks   1960
Rocky Mountain Poems   1960
Sift in an Hourglass   1966
Ixion's Wheel   1969
Selected Poems   1972
Theme & Variations for Sounding Brass   1972
Fire on Stone   1974
Corners in the Glass   1977
Soviet Poems   1978
Sequences   1979
Landscape with Rain   1980
Conflicts of Spring   1981
Gradations of Grandeur   1982
The Moment Is All: Selected Poems 1944-83
Solidarnošč: Prelude   1983
At the Ocean's Verge   1984
Directives of Autumn   1984
Impromptus   1984
Twelve Landscapes   1985
Manipulations on Greek Themes   1987

Short Stories

The Brazen Tower   1974
The Vivid Air   1980

Also by Ralph Gustafson

Poetry

The Golden Chalice   1935
Alfred the Great   1937
Epithalamium in Time of War   1941
Lyrics Unromantic   1942
Flight into Darkness   1944
Rivers among Rocks   1960
Rocky Mountain Poems   1960
Sift in an Hourglass   1966
Ixion's Wheel   1969
Selected Poems   1972
Theme & Variations for Sounding Brass   1972
Fire on Stone   1974
Corners in the Glass   1977
Soviet Poems   1978
Sequences   1979
Landscape with Rain   1980
Conflicts of Spring   1981
Gradations of Grandeur   1982
The Moment Is All: Selected Poems 1944-83
Solidarnošč: Prelude   1983
At the Ocean's Verge   1984
Directives of Autumn   1984
Impromptus   1984
Twelve Landscapes   1985
Manipulations on Greek Themes   1987

Short Stories

The Brazen Tower   1974
The Vivid Air   1980

Essays

Plummets & Other Partialities   1987

Letters

A Literary Friendship:
The Correspondence of Ralph Gustafson and W. W. E. Ross   *1984*

Anthologies (as editor)

Pelican Anthology of Canadian Poetry   1942
A Little Anthology of Canadian Poets   1943
Canadian Accent   1944
The Penguin Book of Canadian Verse   1958, 1967, 1975, 1984